mission-shaped
children

moving towards a child-centred Church

Margaret Withers

CHURCH HOUSE
PUBLISHING

Church House Publishing
Church House
Great Smith Street
London SW1P 3AZ

978-0-7151-4232-5

Published 2006 by Church House Publishing

Third impression 2010

Copyright © The Archbishops' Council 2006

The opinions expressed in this book are those of the
author and do not necessarily reflect the official policy
of the General Synod or The Archbishops' Council of
the Church of England

Cover design by ie Design

Printed by CPI Antony Rowe, Chippenham, Wiltshire

Contents

Series introduction

In adopting and commending the *Mission-shaped Church* report, the Church of England took an important step forward in its understanding of God's mission. It is a journey full of opportunities and challenges, and one which opens up new questions. This series of titles is designed to resource thinking, reflection and action as the journey continues.

Each title in the *Mission-shaped series* considers how the principles presented in *Mission-shaped Church* can be applied in different areas of the Church's life and mission – in work with children and young people, in rural areas, in the parish church and in the area of apostolic spirituality. What perspectives, and inner values are necessary to be part of a mission-shaped Church today? These areas were touched upon in the MSC report but are now explored in more depth.

All the authors write with the benefit of years of practical experience. The real-life case studies and practical examples they provide are designed both to be inspirational models of ministry and mission and to be adapted by the reader for their own context.

The examples cited include both 'fresh expressions', developed as a response to the culture of a particular group of people, and more traditional models, reflecting the fact that 'there are many ways in which the reality of "church" can exist'.* This series is firmly committed to advocating a mixed economy model for the church of the future.

---

*Archbishop Rowan Williams, from the Foreword to *Mission-shaped Church*.

Foreword

Margaret Withers has done the whole Church of England a service by applying the strategies of *Mission-shaped church* to the Church's ministry with children. The insights in this book will help the church regain both hope and vision for its mission among children. The church has more existing opportunities for outreach with children than is often recognized: both on Sundays and midweek, in parish premises and its schools. The current climate of permission for imaginative mission initiatives and fresh expressions of church, also opens up new possibilities. Child-centred ministry can be a key component of the mixed economy church.

This book challenges us to explore what it means for children to be church, and to own and celebrate the many ways children are engaging with faith issues beyond the Sunday service, like in the all-age community of the school. I (Jackie) find this both challenging and exciting. It is the world I inhabit daily and where I witness a growing community of faith, the school's witness to Christian values in the local community. Last but not least the impact on the local church where a new 'family' service has recently been started because of the children's experience of 'being church' in the school context.

Our children need an opportunity to be genuine members of our communities of faith and we do need to recognise that children are already an integral part of the Church's mission in the world. I hope this book will stimulate and challenge our thinking and years of reflecting into action for the honour and sake of the health of God's Church.

Revd Jackie Cray previously Families and under-5s Adviser for CPAS
Bishop Graham Cray, Chairman of the Mission-shaped Church *working party*

Acknowledgements

This response to *Mission-shaped Church* could not have been written without the support of colleagues who share my passion for a Church where children are seen to be part of its mission.

In particular, I wish to thank the following people who allowed me to interview them or who sent me their stories:

Antony Homer, *Being church at school*

Rona Orme, *Celebrating together in a rural benefice*

Charlotte Nobbs, *Children at Grange Park church*

Fran Papantoniou, *Church to school and back again*

Howard Cocks, *Evangelism through music*

Claire Johnson, *ExCELLent*

Peter Clark, *Kidz Klub at Page Moss, Liverpool*

Lucy Moore, *Messy Church at Cowplain*

Richard Beadle, *Praise & Play on Sunday morning*

Simon Marsh, *Parish Power*

Janet Marshall, *Pilgrimage, a journey into faith*

Heather Waldsax, *Praying together*

Jane Whitcombe, *Scratch nativity*

Robert Beaken, *Squeals on wheels*

James Southward, *The God-Bods*

John Peal, *The village wedding*

Rosie Tallowin, *What is church for you?*

The Lion's Den and Being church at school were originally written for the Fresh Expressions' web site and are reproduced with permission. *The Church went to the children* first appeared as a longer article in *Country Way.*[1] These and all the other stories are drawn from my own experience, through my work and just listening to people anywhere, including at parties and on trains. I have attempted to ensure accuracy whenever possible.

Thanks are also due to Anne Richards, Cinde Lee, John Hall, Paul Bayes and Rona Orme for reading and commenting on the manuscript, and especially to Tracey Messenger, commissioning editor for Church House Publishing, who guided me throughout and ensured that I reached the deadline date.

Introduction: the child at the centre of the Church

One Sunday in September 2005, I attended a Harvest Thanksgiving Eucharist at a church in a small town on the coast. It was very different from the usual harvest service. Firstly, as it took place in a seaside parish, the theme was thanking God for the harvest of the sea, remembering the fisherfolk, lifeboat crews and members of the Royal and the Merchant Navy who worked on it to bring us our food and ensure our safety. The service ended with the congregation processing to the beach for the blessing of the sea next to the fishing boats, the harbour and the lifeboat station. Secondly, and equally significant, the whole service was led by about 25 children with a handful of teachers to support them. They served, provided the music, wrote and read all the prayers, acted the Gospel and sermon, and presented the gifts at the Offertory. The priest greeted the people, said the eucharistic prayer and gave a blessing.

The Gospel used in that service was Luke's account of the shoal of fish, and Jesus' call to Simon Peter, 'Don't be afraid; from now on you will be catching people' (Luke 5.10, NRSV). Clergy and readers will have preached on it. Children's leaders will have taught it and the activity probably included the children making brightly coloured fish with their names on, to put in some kind of net. The image of being 'caught' by Jesus and remaining safe in his net – his Church – is a powerful one.

There is, however, a darker side to this analogy of catching people as if they were fish. Fish are food. They are caught so that they can be killed and eaten. People, on the other hand, are not food but feeders. They are 'caught' by Jesus; they feed on his Word and sacraments and, in turn, catch other feeders. It is called making new disciples.

There is a tendency for the Church subconsciously to treat children like fish: goods to be used to fill the gaps in the pews so that the Church is safe for the future, rather like stocking up the freezer before heavy snow, or filling the car with petrol before yet another price rise. Too often, nurture and worship for children are about containing and entertaining, like keeping fish in a net, rather than engaging with and growing young Christians who can move freely and give as much as they receive.

For the last 60 years, the number of children attending church or Sunday school has fallen steadily, but scant attention has been given to recognizing that children are a growing and vital part of the Church's mission in other ways. The Church of England's report, *Mission-shaped Church*[1] mentions children in passing several times, but only as passive beings, or fish caught in nets. Constraints of space prevented it from exploring the enormous contribution that children make to the traditional church, and it did not cover the diversity of ways that children are being church beyond Sunday morning.

In the Church of England alone, thousands of children are meeting to worship God and hear the good news in ways beyond the traditional Sunday morning service.

The aims of this book are twofold. First, if a review of the Church as a community is to be balanced, it must include every generation, so it is written as a response to *Mission-shaped Church* from the perspective of children. The first three chapters consider the changes in society that have led to a transformation in the way that children live today. They re-examine that rich heritage of Christian educational pioneers who set the basis for universal free education for children, its subsequent secularization, but then its recent recovery of awareness of children as beings who need to experience and develop the spiritual dimension of life through religious tradition and practice.

Second, this book shows how children are part of the Church's mission: how they worship God throughout the week, witness to their faith, as well as having, in many instances, a vibrant ministry in the traditional church setting. This is not necessarily about doing different things, but about using what we have better and making it more inclusive. Contrary to media reports and anecdotal evidence, children do attend church. They come on Sunday mornings, to special services, on family occasions like baptisms, weddings and funerals, and they come to church with their schools for celebrations, lessons and other events. The quality of welcome and worship they find will play a large part in their deciding whether they want to come to that church, or indeed any church, again.

Children are also worshipping God at other times than the usual Sunday services. They range from groups of toddlers with their parents or carers, to midweek worship, to a club operating on Saturday morning. Many Church schools are distinctive Christian communities with worship at the centre of everything they do. The Church meets children (and sometimes their parents) where they are, in every sense, and these meetings and events are frequently highly successful both numerically and as a Christian witness in the community. The Church needs to celebrate and resource these occasions as equal and valuable forms of worship that help youngsters to build a relationship with God and be part of a Christian community.

This book is designed to help you to see that many children are already an integral part of the traditional church and how others are meeting to worship God in a variety of ways, some of which are hardly noticed.

Chapters 1–3

The first three chapters relate closely to *Mission-shaped Church*.

Chapter 1 gives an overview of how some of the cultural, social and economic changes of the last 30 years have had an impact on the lives of children.

Chapter 2 considers how the Church has provided for children over the last century, Christian education, the growth and subsequent demise of the Sunday school movement and what followed it.

In **Chapter 3** we look at the complex pattern that makes up many children's contact with the Christian faith today and define some of the obstacles that can stand in the way of an active ministry among children.

Chapters 4–9

These chapters explore some of the many ways in which children are being church, from Sunday morning, midweek and beyond the church walls.

Chapter 4 looks at how the traditional church can engage with children, and the possibilities for development.

Chapter 5 shows the characteristics of ways in which children are meeting as new and risky church.

Chapter 6 demonstrates how many children's groups are becoming new forms of church.

Chapter 7 considers some of the joys and challenges of churches moving towards being all-age worshipping communities.

Many schools are already all-age worshipping communities – **Chapter 8** looks at schools as part of the Church's mission in the community.

Chapter 9 presents examples of children's being church at some distance from the church building, for example on Christian holidays.

Having built up a picture of infinite variety, **Chapter 10** considers how each church can respond to the challenge of being a child-shaped church.

Further sources of information and a reading list are given at the end of the book.

The **stories,** and the **questions for discussion** at the end of each chapter, are there to help you to review how children may already be part of your own worshipping community, and how this can be sustained and developed further. You may find these helpful if you are reading the book as a small group, with your PCC or with a team of children's workers.

This book does not prescribe any one model or a right way to do things. The questions are there to help you think through your own situation, and to encourage you to start from where you are. Any church can have a valuable ministry with children, even if it is small in numbers. Indeed, many of the stories in this book show how small and sometimes struggling churches have been given new life and hope through their 'mission-shaped' children.

That harvest service beside the sea was a powerful reminder of the valuable ministry of children and how much they can give to us if we will allow them the opportunity. Our ministry with children should not be regarded as an 'insurance policy' for the Church – that is, a way of ensuring that they will eventually become fully paid-up members and guarantee its future. Children are a blessing, an integral part of the Church of today, and a sign of the kingdom of God among us.

More changes than at any other time in history: children's life and culture

1. Recent social trends and their effect on children

This chapter considers the impact of recent cultural, social and economic trends on the lives of children. Many of these changes are described in chapter 1 of *Mission-shaped Church*. The last 20 years have seen more changes in a child's life than any other time in history. The world has been through the fastest technical revolution that has ever happened in the life of this planet, with accompanying changes in lifestyle and economy. British society has been no exception.

The resulting upheaval has affected everyone, but children's lives have been changed the most. It cannot be assumed that the effects of such changes on children are similar to those experienced by adults. In some instances, as the stories in this chapter demonstrate, they are markedly different.

The final section of this chapter explores the challenges and opportunities that these changes present to the Church as it attempts to engage with children.

2. Employment changes

> Most people in their middle years work outside the home . . .
> There has been a significant increase in the number of lone parent women working outside the home . . . The hours worked have also changed.[1]

> **story**
> **story**
> **story**
> **story**
>
> ## Being a family together
>
> David and Carol both work in retail management.
> In order to cover the care for their children, Carol
> works an early morning shift. This starts at 6.30 a.m. and ends
> at 2.30 p.m., while David usually finishes work at about 7.30
> in the evening. So, the whole family is rarely together. After
> discussion, David has applied to work on only one Sunday
> each month so that they can spend the day as a family.

As this example demonstrates, the pattern of working a five-day week from
9 a.m. to 5 p.m., or similar hours, which was common until the 1980s, has
radically changed. More service industries operate throughout the whole
week. Twenty-four hour call-centres, garages and supermarkets, fast-food
outlets, Sunday trading and extended licensing laws have become the norm.
Flexible working, shift work and job sharing are widespread.

Government initiatives have encouraged lone parents to support
themselves, leading to a vast increase in the number in full-time employment.
Even more lone parents with children aged below five years are taking
part-time or full-time work.[2]

Although legislation prevents people being required to work for more than
48 hours each week, a substantial number work for over 50 hours a week.
Some workers spend the whole week in the city centre and travel home to
their families for weekends. It is reported that the largest number of second
homes in the UK are small flats in or near central London. At the other end
of the economic spectrum, people work long hours because the hourly rate
of pay is low, they are self-employed, or they have a number of low paid
part-time jobs.

The combination of these factors has lessened the time that whole families
can spend together. The increase in flexible working hours has led to some
parents working in different shifts in order to cover childcare. More young
children are cared for by childminders or in nurseries.[3] There is a marked
increase in demand for places in after-school clubs.[4] The government has
recently (June 2005) announced plans for extended school days to increase
and to regularize this care service.

The number of families sharing meals regularly has lessened, so there is less free time for discussion of the school day, interests and needs. If Sunday is a work-free day, it is kept for family matters: shopping, sports, DIY, or visiting friends and relations.

3.   Mobility

Today people are vastly more mobile than they were even 30 years ago . . . Most families, apart from the poorest, have access to a car, and are ready to use it.[5]

A large number of children are taken to school by car. Some parents may drop their children off on the way to work, but cars are also used so children can avoid having to cross main roads, as a substitute for inadequate public transport, to save time, and to avoid 'stranger danger' – parents being worried about their children being out by themselves. It also enables parents to 'shop around' for schools or children's activities that are a distance from home. In a few cases, a child may go to school near to a parent's place of work rather than that nearest to home.

The ensuing problems of lack of exercise are well documented but there are also social disadvantages: lack of contact with friends on the journey, dependence on the goodwill of busy parents, and less opportunity to walk in the locality. This limits the opportunity to develop independence through walking to visit friends or local shops and eventually travelling on public transport.

At weekends, families are able to enjoy outings or visit relations and friends some distance from home. If they attend a church, it can be the one of their choice, maybe as far as 30 miles away, rather than the nearest one. This allows families to seek out a church where children are made welcome and there is good quality children's ministry. It can also lead to numerous car journeys when the children develop friendships and interests connected with the church.

4.   Divorce and changes in family life

> The divorce rate has gone up significantly . . . Combined with
> the rise of cohabitation and the birth of children to never-
> married mothers, in 2001 the Census showed that 22 per
> cent of children . . . live in lone parent families . . . More than
> 1 in 10 other children live in stepfamilies. The average age of
> women at the birth of their first child has increased . . . to 27
> years in 2000.[6]

The implications of these changes are vast and affect children the most. If
separated or divorced parents live close to each other, children may share
time between their parents, splitting the week, or spending time between
school and bedtime with one parent while living with the other. Other
children will spend weekends or holiday time with the second parent and
maybe an entire second family. This makes it very difficult for such children
to sustain friendships outside school or attend a particular church each
week, even if the parents are practising Christians.

The rise in the age at which women are having children means that many
women have had satisfying careers before starting their families and find
parenthood very isolating. As noted above, many mothers of young children
return to work and their children are cared for in nurseries or by
childminders. The demand for activities or clubs for children under five
years stems from the Government's moves to expand nursery and
preschool provision. It has had the added benefit of providing a place
where young parents and carers can meet socially and discuss matters
concerning the children in their care.

5.   Free time

> Taking part in sporting activities, whether alone or as a
> member of a team or club, is a popular way of spending
> leisure time . . . The biggest change in leisure time in the past
> 50 years has been in the hours spent watching television.[7]

Many sporting events involving children take place on Sundays as well as
on Saturdays or after school. These include swimming, five-a-side football,

dancing, horse riding, playing in school teams and watching football matches. Some popular schools demand this sort of participation as a condition of entry, so attending church on Sunday can become a casualty of going to a particular school.

With the advent of satellite and digital television, the number of television channels available has expanded from four to well over a hundred in the last 20 years. The price of television sets has reduced so that some children are able to have their own set in their bedroom, and possibly a video or DVD player as well.

The biggest change, however, in the way that children spend their free time has taken place during the last ten years with the development of computers and the inclusion of ICT in the school curriculum. Every child has access to a computer at school and 53 per cent of households possessed one in 2004–5.[8] Children use the Internet to find information, play games and communicate with friends and people all over the world. They play at home and go to computer clubs. Hand-held computer games are plentiful. An article in *The Guardian* reported in April 2004 that, in 2001, 13 per cent of primary school-aged children owned a mobile phone. This had risen to 25 per cent by the beginning of 2004.[9]

6.   A fragmented society

> One key conclusion . . . is that we are living increasingly
> fragmented lives . . . . People no longer view Sunday as special,
> or as 'church time'. Children are more likely to be playing
> sport than being in Sunday school or church.[10]

Drawing together some of the accounts in previous sections of children's lives, we find a way of life that was almost unknown 20 years ago.

Children may live some distance from grandparents and other relations. They will travel to visit them at weekends and during the school holidays but may only see them occasionally. A substantial number of children will live with one parent (usually the mother) but spend time with the other parent and, possibly, a whole second family. This will effectively give them two homes and sets of people, lifestyles and values.

If children travel to school by car, they may not know their own locality or neighbours, or be capable of making their own way between home and school.

As a large number of children's mothers work either full- or part-time, some children will spend the time before and after school at a childminder's home. Others will attend breakfast and after-school clubs at school or in a community centre. This pattern may vary according to the day of the week or the hours of the parent's work.

Many of the children being born into this society will know no other way of living. The communities where families still live close to each other and where grandparents play a vital role in the upbringing and care of children are declining as society becomes increasingly mobile. Children will form a multiplicity of networks of friends through school and other activities that may have few people in common. Whereas a child would have called at a friend's home or 'phoned for a chat 20 years ago, he or she is just as likely to use text messaging or email today.

7. Consumer culture and the effect on children

The effects of bringing up children in such a consumer culture are well known and documented. One obvious side effect is the shortening of childhood. Even the youngest children are dressed as miniature adults with the consequent expectation that they will behave accordingly. Another is the constant pressure to possess the latest computer toy, film-related merchandise or football strip. An image-obsessed culture is having a negative effect on some children's sense of self-worth. As well as demanding special clothes and hairstyles to look like their sporting or pop idols, an increasing number of young children are thinking that they are 'fat' or 'ugly' and thus developing eating disorders or even wanting plastic surgery to change their bodies.

The picture described in this chapter is one of busy families squeezing time together in a crowded day, spending weekends visiting relations, doing DIY and enjoying sports and leisure together. It has been pointed out that this is achieved only by being flexible and mobile, 'Most families, apart from the poorest, have access to a car . . .'[11] But what of the poorest families? What is today's society like for the children who live below the 'breadline'?

8.   Childhood poverty

If children are victims of long-term unemployment, poor housing and the poverty associated with such deprivation, they soon become acutely aware that they lack many of the good things that are enjoyed by other children, maybe even those in the same class at school. This can be seen to run counter to today's consumerist culture and almost treated as a virtue by those who observe it but do not have to experience the negative effects that lack of choice can have on children. At an extreme level, deprivation as basic as not having proper school uniform, living in cramped temporary accommodation, or being unable to visit a local attraction because there is not a bus service, is real and diminishing to children's well-being. This is exacerbated by many of the poorest children being brought up by a lone parent who is struggling to provide the necessities of life.

Reality of poverty

Donna was thirteen. She was always very late for school on Mondays and missed most of the first lesson. Her mother worked as an office cleaner early in the morning so Donna had to get breakfast for her younger brothers and sisters and take them to school each day. On Mondays, she then had to wait for the Post Office to open in order to collect the child allowance, as there was rarely enough money left from the previous week to pay her bus fare to school.

It is generally accepted that the gap between the richest and poorest families has grown during the last 30 years. This is not confined to certain parts of the country or to the inner cities. For example, the introduction of the minimum wage doubled the earnings of some agricultural workers and led to unemployment for others. Unlike previous generations, there is no way of shielding children from the physical effects of affluence. Television advertisements, the Internet, and media coverage of the lives of celebrities have thrust a glamorous picture of material comfort into every child's home. They see captivating clothes, toys, interests and lifestyles at the press of a button and notice them being enjoyed by some of their better off companions.

9. Legislation: the Children Act

In the last 20 years, legislation has transformed the care and well-being of children. The Children Act (1989) was the biggest piece of legislation concerning children for over a century. It made the welfare of children paramount in the home, school and the wider community. This has led to child protection legislation and guidelines that affect every contact with a child, whether in school or through voluntary agencies, including the Church.

The Church of England has developed a child protection policy,[12] and dioceses provide training and Criminal Records Bureau (CRB) checks for those who have a ministry among children. This has, in its turn, forced Parochial Church Councils (PCCs) to recognize their responsibility for the management and nurture of the children in their care. Some churches have risen to the challenge by providing higher standards of nurture and more training for children's leaders.

The Government's policy of providing 'wrap-around childcare' with registration of child minders, and childcare facilities, and the recent introduction of Children's Centres in every area have provided ways of ensuring that children's medical, social and educational needs are catered for through a single scheme of care. Local Authorities have responded by setting up Early Years Development and Childcare forums that include representatives of faith groups. Much of their work has been involved with setting up preschools, holiday clubs, after-school activities and even breakfast clubs and providing training for people who have care of children whether childminders, playscheme leaders or working in statutory education.

The effect has been a general raising of standards of childcare and a heightening of awareness of the value of work with children, whether professional or as a volunteer. It has also presented the Church with opportunities for outreach to children in the community through establishing its own groups or allowing them to operate on church premises.

10. Education

Alongside legislation on childcare, educational legislation has transformed the whole education system. Officially, there is more parental choice and the establishment of Technology Colleges (now called Specialist Schools), and Academies has further expanded choice at secondary level. This has had a corresponding knock-on effect on younger children.

Since the national curriculum was established in 1989, followed by regular inspections of schools by OFSTED, there have been enormous changes in the way that children are taught and expected to learn. Children's progress is regularly tested, and since 1997 there has been a renewed stress on the basic skills of literacy and numeracy. Science and information and communication technology (ICT) have become core subjects, with citizenship also compulsory at secondary level since 2002. In addition, students have lessons in personal, social and health education (PSHE).

Many teachers and children have responded well to the challenges, but creative subjects like music and drama are being squeezed out, and lack of time and space to play may be a factor in some of the increased behavioural difficulties in quite young children. There is currently considerable worry that the lack of time and space for sports is affecting children's health. This is exacerbated by the rise in use of fast foods and the number of children who travel by car and would rather play with computers than an active game in the garden or street.

The Church has a role to play in challenging these trends in its service in the community. Some churches or Church schools are running breakfast clubs to ensure that children have a nourishing meal at the beginning of the day. Those that are held in an urban parish where the children attend several different schools may offer a 'walking bus' service to escort the children to school. There is a development of five-a-side football clubs with matches being held between parishes on Sunday after the church service. Some churches can also encourage development of the creative arts by offering their premises for music, drama and craft clubs. This is discussed further in Chapter 6.

Spiritual and moral development have been officially recognized as an intrinsic part of a child's formation since 1944. They are now, with social and cultural development, inspected by OFSTED alongside the quality of teaching and learning. At the same time, there is a new openness to children's learning about religions and experiencing worship. Most schools will welcome help from members of faith communities. Changes in RE have presented opportunities for children to visit local churches as part of their studies and take part in acts of worship. Many Church schools have responded to the changes in inspection and curriculum and to the Dearing review[13] by becoming more consciously Christian. Corporate acts of worship have to be planned and recorded. About 50 per cent of Church schools have eucharistic worship at some time during the school year.

11. Post-Christendom

Much of Britain's self-understanding comes from centuries of Christian faith, but ... the Christian story is no longer at the heart of the nation ... Among some young people there is little evidence of any belief in a transcendent dimension.[14]

In December 2000, an article appeared in *The Spectator* entitled 'Mummy, why are all those people kneeling?' In it, the writer (an agnostic) expressed a concern that her children were not hearing the Christian story and that the nation was in danger of losing its cultural heritage. The worry that it can no longer be guaranteed that anyone born since 1950 will know anything about the Christian faith, including the meaning of Christmas and Easter, has gone far beyond the Christian community. A creeping secularization has all but destroyed many of the Christian symbols that served as silent witnesses in society. Some local authorities have banned the erection of Christmas cribs in public places and there has recently been considerable discussion about the removal of a large cross from a crematorium. Biblical metaphor that was common currency: a 'mote and beam' situation, 'sufficient unto the day', and so on, is all but meaningless, with a knock-on effect on the reading of much of our English literature.

The traditional, picture-postcard image of a church in the centre of a village community is unrelated to almost any child's lifestyle. If church exists at all, it will be one of many factors on the edge of a busy life.

Referring to the *UK Christian Handbook*,[15] *Mission-shaped Church* states:

> During the twentieth century Sunday school attendance
> dropped from 55 per cent to 4 per cent of children, meaning
> that even the rudiments of the Christian story and of
> Christian experience are lacking in most young people.[16]

These figures demonstrate a serious decline in what used to be the mainstay of Christian nurture. As Sunday school is not, however, the sole means of nurturing children, the picture is not as grim as is suggested. About 20 per cent of the nation's children are educated in Anglican primary schools. A further 10 per cent are educated in Roman Catholic schools. Some churches reach out to children through holiday and midweek clubs. Evangelistic organizations such as the Church Army run missions and camps, work in schools and clubs, and spearhead new parish developments that include children. The opportunities are there for substantial numbers of children to learn about the Christian faith and experience Christian worship within a Christian community. It is important that the teaching is seen by the children to be relevant to their own lives, and that the church can help children to develop that childhood faith as the young person matures in a post-Christian society.

12.   Where are the children?

The picture presented here is one of contradictions. Children live in a fast-moving fragmented society, but their lives are highly structured. Many children enjoy affluence that was unknown a generation ago, but the poorest are not only poorer but are also acutely aware of the increasing gap between them and their peers.

Children will probably spend less time with their parents than a generation ago. Not only will their parents be working, but their children will also have a wide variety of entertainment through television and computers in their homes, and maybe in their bedrooms. Sunday may be a family day, but it will probably be structured with shopping, visiting relations, sports and entertainment. The time to enjoy each other's company, to talk through interests, new discoveries or problems is very limited.

Most children are well cared for by a variety of carers as well as parents and teachers. In one sense, this has replaced the extended family. Legislation has ensured that their well-being is paramount. The school week may be complex, with different people dropping off and picking up, and maybe some evenings spent at a childminder's home or a club.

According to *Mission-shaped Church*, most families, apart from the poorest, have access to a car.[17] It follows that most children travel by car regularly. This allows them to enjoy entertainment or activities a distance from home, but it makes them dependent on their parents' availability and goodwill. Many children have little experience of walking around their local neighbourhood and the growing independence and sense of adventure that accompanies it.

Children are consumers. They are targeted by the clothes and toy markets and can expect everything in their lives to be tailor-made to suit their needs. This includes their education and their religion. Families can seek out a church that fits their needs rather than worshipping in the local community. The 'Child Friendly Church Award' in the diocese of Liverpool is a case in point. It has broken new ground by focusing on the importance of churches' welcoming and nurturing children, and helps new families to see where there will be a high standard of worship and nurture for children.

Children will read books and see films featuring the spiritual world of Harry Potter and Star Wars. Some of the stories, such as C. S. Lewis's *The Lion, the Witch and the Wardrobe* will have a story that can be linked with Christianity. Others will portray the Church in a negative light. RE lessons will explore the faith and practice of the Christian and other religions and will probably include visiting a church and joining in acts of worship. Yet, few children will have any meaningful understanding of organized religion. Fewer still will come to know the personal love of God for each one of us and experience what it is to be a valued member of a Christian community.

13.   From 'where?' to 'how?'

Mission-shaped Church states:

> Anglicans aim to follow the pattern of the incarnation – to be with people where they are, how they are. The word 'where' in that sentence suggests geography and territory – being in a

particular place and location. In Britain today, it might help
to say that we must be with people *how* they are. 'How' is a
word that suggests connection beyond geography and locality
– connecting with people's culture, values, lifestyle and
networks, as well as with their location.[18]

If we alter one word in that statement, we get a challenging picture:

> Anglicans aim . . . to be with *children* where they are, how
> they are . . . In Britain today, it might help to say that we must
> be with *children how* they are . . . connecting with *children's*
> culture, values, lifestyle and networks, as well as with their
> location. (Author's italics.)

The tradition of seeing children's ministry as their attending church or
Sunday school has been unproductive for at least 50 years. However, it is
still the expectation of many parishes. Children's ministry, more often called
'children's work', is considered as a nurture programme that happens on
Sunday morning in the church building or a hall nearby. There are, however,
many other ways that children meet to explore the Christian faith and,
indeed, to be 'church'. Many of them are almost unnoticed and are not
seen as integral to the parish's mission in the community. Some have to
be self-funding.

The diversity of ways that children are being church forms the basis of this
book. The range in style of worship, place and way of engaging with the
children is huge. The three things they have in common are that they are
numerically successful, they reach children who would not normally have
anything to do with a traditional church, and they meet the children 'where
they are' in every sense.

Mission-shaped Church correctly points out that the new is not necessarily
better or more lasting.[19] The various ways in which children are 'being
church' beyond Sunday morning may appear to be 'new'. They are in
essence, however, a recovery of the spirit and methods of the Sunday
school pioneers of the early nineteenth century who reached out to the
children who worked in the mills, then ran in the streets on Sunday.

14. Opportunity and repentance

This is, indeed, a moment of opportunity and of repentance.

> If the decline of the Church is ultimately caused neither by the
> irrelevance of Jesus, nor by the indifference of the community,
> but by the Church's failure to respond fast enough to an
> evolving culture, to a changing spiritual climate, and the
> promptings of the Holy Spirit, then that decline can be
> addressed by the repentance of the Church.[20]

In June 2005, the diocese of Birmingham, celebrating its centenary, held a
festal service in its cathedral – 'Celebrating Children'. Bishop Sentamu[21]
reminded the assembled congregation that, in 1905, every working class
child went to Sunday school. 'That must be hard to imagine,' he said. The
packed cathedral watched film clips of processions of children and their
teachers at Sunday school events, in the open air, without a church building
in sight. Most of them were clearly enjoying themselves: a few pulled faces
at the camera! After the film, the bishop spoke again, 'Can you make that
happen again?' he asked. Around the cathedral, came a whispered, 'Yes'.

Some questions for discussion

1. Over the last 20 years, what have been the
    major changes in children's lives? Are there any
    changes that particularly relate to the children
    in your community?

2. What are the needs of the children in your community? Make a list
    of them. Are they ones that the church takes into account when
    planning its children's ministry?

3. Take a wide piece of paper. Divide it into four columns. Head them:
    Church group, Church links, No connection, Not happening. Using the list
    from question 2, make a profile of your church's outreach to children
    by putting each item into one of the columns. Add any other
    children's activities that happen in your community. Look at each
    column in turn. Are your church activities going well? Could your
    church make links with non-church groups? Is there a glaring gap,

such as no family or youth worship, or nothing for young children and their families?

4.   This is a time of repentance. Have we allowed our children's work to become dull and lacklustre? Do we try to engage with children where they are in every sense – or do we want them to be as we were 40 years ago? Do we resource our children's work adequately?

5.   This is a time of opportunity. Do we look at our ministry among children as being something that happens on Sunday? Are there other ways in which the children in our community are worshipping God or learning about the Christian faith? Do we acknowledge and support them?

2 Nurturing Christian children: the last one hundred years

The first chapter concluded with a challenge to the children's leaders of Birmingham to revive the vision of the Sunday school movement of the beginning of the last century. This chapter reviews the story of children and the Church in the last one hundred years. It focuses on the huge changes since the demise of the traditional Sunday school and the challenges the Church has to address as it struggles to re-engage with children and their parents who have little, if any, familiarity with the Christian faith in practice. Today, many children are learning and experiencing the Christian faith in other ways and places besides Sunday in church, and there is a growing appreciation that these forms of outreach need to be owned and resourced by the local and wider Church.

1. Sunday school and the beginnings of universal education

It is often assumed that every child attended Sunday school, church or chapel in the first years of the twentieth century. This was not necessarily the case, but, as it is demonstrated in the following paragraphs, nearly every child had some teaching about the Christian faith and some of this stemmed from Sunday school.

Sunday schools had developed during the industrial revolution, when they provided basic education for the children who worked in the factories and mills. The aim of Robert Raikes, the journalist and philanthropist who founded the first Sunday school in 1780, was to teach children who worked in factories to read the Bible and live by the values it taught. The practice of religion had been in decline and the Sunday school movement was to become the greatest evangelistic movement in this country since the Reformation. It was also the beginning of free education for all.

In 1811, the National Society for the Education of the Poor in the Principles of the Established Church throughout England and Wales was founded.[1] Its purpose was: 'that the National Religion should be made the foundation of National Education, and should be the first and chief thing taught to the poor, according to the excellent Liturgy and Catechism provided by our Church.'[2] The mission of the Society was to found a Church school in every parish. By the end of the nineteenth century, about 50 per cent of children were educated in schools run by the National Society (known as 'national schools') and similar denominational bodies. They were collectively known as 'voluntary schools'.

In 1870, the Forster Education Act divided the country into 2,500 districts. Local ratepayers elected School Boards to examine the provision of education provided by the voluntary societies, and, where it was found to be inadequate, to build and maintain further schools out of the rates. Religious teaching was non-denominational, and, in some cases, left to the Sunday schools, which turned their attention to providing basic Christian teaching for children who did not come to church.

The politician and reformer Philip Snowden wrote about the newly formed board school he attended in about 1874:

> We were not troubled with the religious question, for, in order to avoid all controversy, the Board from the beginning banished the Bible from the school, not because they were irreligious, but because they believed that the teaching of religion was best carried out by the sects in their own Sunday Schools.[3]

By 1900, every child had to be educated up to the age of twelve years and children from the poorest families did not pay fees. According to Christian Research's statistics, 55 per cent of children attended Sunday school.[4] Some other children, usually from middle class families, attended church. Owing to its history of providing education for the poor, Sunday school was often considered to be for working class children whose parents did not attend church.

Enrolled at birth

Kath was baptized as a baby and enrolled into the Sunday school at the same time at St Peter's Walworth in South London in 1920. This was the usual practice. The curate visited each family when the baptized children were about four years old and they were expected to take up their membership of the Sunday school.

2.   Varied ways of reaching out to children

The Sunday school, though the foremost way of teaching children about the faith, was only one aspect of the Church's mission among children. The entire State educational system was based on Christian culture and practice. Young people from wealthy families were educated at public schools, mostly with a strong Anglican ethos, attended daily worship in chapel and were prepared for confirmation as a matter of course. The links between the Anglican voluntary schools and their local churches were strong, with the curate teaching RE and diocesan exams from an early age[5]. Boys were recruited into church choirs, and, in churches of the Anglo-Catholic tradition, as servers. This gave them experience of the *Book of Common Prayer* with its collects and large portions of Scripture, including the psalms. It also gave them a place as part of the worshipping community.

Charles's Sunday

Charles Godden, a coachman's son and a friend of the author's family, recalled some years ago his childhood Sundays at Chiddingly church in Sussex before the First World War.

'I went to church to sing in the choir in the morning. We had to have learned the collect, and recite it before the service. In the afternoon, it was Sunday school, then home to tea. Then I went back to church again to sing in the evening.'

The development of uniformed organizations such as the Boy's Brigade, in 1883, founded to provide a more active Christian education than Sunday school, followed by the Boy Scout movement in 1907 with its promise to 'do my duty to God . . .', with their companion organizations for girls, provided activities with a strong Christian background for children and young people. Regular church parades strengthened links with the church and its worship. Crusaders and similar groups flourished, providing biblical teaching and the camaraderie of summer camps where young people lived and worshipped with fellow Christians of their own age. The Church Army and other evangelistic organizations ran beach missions to evangelize the growing numbers of children whose families took holidays in seaside resorts.

3.   Structured Sunday school teaching

As Sunday schools focused on teaching the Christian faith to unchurched children, the Sunday School Union, (now Christian Education) the National Society and other organizations established education councils and training courses, with Scripture examinations and certificates for children. Large numbers of children[6] attended Sunday school to learn Bible stories, pray the Lord's Prayer and sing well-known hymns. They memorized the Ten Commandments, a weekly biblical text and collect, and the values and language they learned became part of everyday currency.

Numbers were falling, but were large enough for the established models to remain virtually unchanged until after the Second World War. Sunday schools followed the educational model with classes and examinations, with children having little, if any, experience of being part of a worshipping community or of contact with an adult congregation.

4.   A rapidly changing world

In 1944, the Butler Education Act made radical changes to state education, which had a major effect on Sunday school and churchgoing for young people. The school leaving age was raised to fifteen. The schools where most children had stayed throughout their school careers became primary schools and every child moved to a secondary school at the age of eleven. As the children left their local primary school, they also discarded Sunday school as being part of their childish past.[7] Some of them kept contact with the church through uniformed organizations and youth clubs, but many more did not.

Sunday schools continued in the same style, while the world moved on and the numbers shrank. Families who had lost their homes during the Second World War were moved from their close communities, with relations and neighbours to lend a hand or provide friendship, into new housing estates built on the edge of towns. These presented enormous social challenges. Local authorities gave priority for housing to families with children so these estates lacked social diversity: full of young children for a decade, then becoming a community of teenagers with different needs and issues.

The new estates, some of which had turned small villages into towns, were often classified with titles like 'London overspill'. The original residents often resented the loss of their space and changes to their way of life. The new residents had been uprooted from their relatives and familiar surroundings. Some churches worked hard to engage with families on the estates, but many did not.

story
story
story
story
Excluding a social sector

The new incumbent of a parish in west London discovered that, although the congregation claimed to visit every new resident and to deliver Christmas and Easter cards to every home in the parish, it had never considered including the post-war council estate.

This was in 1981.

As more families could take holidays, and television provided instant entertainment at the flick of a switch, religion, or the traditional practice of it, appeared less and less relevant. Church events, including the annual Sunday school outing, were appreciated by fewer and fewer families. Grandparents who had ensured that their grandchildren attended church lived miles away, so their support and influence was lost. A survey in the diocese of

Worcester in 1972–3 noted a 50 per cent fall in Sunday school attendance after 1950.[8] According to Christian Research, Sunday school attendance had fallen to 14 per cent by 1970 and the number continued to decline.

Society was rapidly becoming secularized and the Christian ethos that underpinned the education system was being questioned. Worship was generally considered to be something for committed individuals and the practice of it in school and children's organizations was actively discouraged. A number of debates took place about the nature of religious education in state schools.

> Ronald Goldman (1964) queried whether the teaching methods then in use in Religious Education were effective. He showed how little understanding some of the children he researched seemed to have, and how antagonistic some were towards the whole process of Christian education. He suggested more relevant approaches, still to Christian education, which came to be implemented in some syllabuses as 'life themes' – themes on homes, friendship, shepherds, bread and so on, each having a clearly defined biblical content.[9]

This was followed in 1970 by the Church of England's 'Durham' report, *The Fourth R*, which stated that the role of the RE teacher was educational, not evangelistic, and had different aims from teaching provided by the local church. RE became increasingly the provision of information about different religions through stories, and disregarded the need for children to know about religious experience and practices. Indeed, some RE teachers saw a child's voicing of his or her religious commitment as being a hindrance to objective teaching of the subject.

5. Creating a time bomb

During the 1970s and early 1980s, individual churches experimented with Family Services, or special children's worship, as ways of addressing the decline in attendance. Numbers continued to fall, and, in line with current thinking about the undesirability of providing religious teaching to children with no particular Christian allegiance, some uniformed organizations and schools severed their links with the local church. *Mission-shaped Church* described the fall-out of this situation as a time bomb.

> We are becoming a nation of non-churched people *in terms of Sunday school contact* . . . Those who were 10 years old in 1950 are now fast approaching retirement, and of them 70 per cent were not in Sunday school. That means that the majority of even the elderly are non-churched. (Author's italics.)[10]

The above statement was written in the context of discussion of the Church of England's practice of relying on 'returnees', those who learned the faith as children and returned as older adults. Bearing in mind the wide variety of ways in which the Church engaged with young people before 1970, the picture presented is somewhat distorted. Daily Christian assembly and RE were still part of every child's education in 1950 and the uniformed organizations, choirs and other church activities reached large numbers of youngsters. Up until about that time, most adults could say the Lord's Prayer and sing a few Christmas carols and well-known hymns at weddings and funerals.

If, however, we look at the statement in the context of the history of children's Christian nurture, we will find a very disturbing picture. Those adults who were ten years old in 1950, whether churched or not, had brought up their children in the 1970s when religion in school and children's organizations was actively discouraged, and the traditional Sunday school had become tired and lacklustre. Children who grew up in a culture that marginalized religion in the 1970s are the parents of today's children, and have, for the most part, little if any experience of the basic knowledge that underpins the Christian faith to pass on to their children. The role of the grandparents, now retired, in recovering and passing on the smattering of the faith that they learned as children, is more vital than it has ever been.

6.   Child-centred legislation

The late 1980s and early 1990s were a time of major change for children, with far-reaching legislation by both the State and the Church. As discussed in Chapter 1 (section 9) The Children Act 1989 placed the well-being of the child at the centre of the legislation and did much to change thinking about the rights of the child as well as improving standards of care.

Subsequent education acts changed the way in which children were taught and transformed the teaching of RE and acts of worship, often called 'assemblies'. Most significantly, the spiritual life of the school and its worship had to be assessed as part of regular OFSTED inspections. As a direct result of the Education Reform Act in 1988, allowing schools to opt out of local authority control and become grant maintained, many Church schools strengthened their links with their diocesan Boards of Education and local churches while controlled schools started to become more consciously Christian as a result of having denominational inspections.

7. Children in the Way

The Church of England's report, *Children in the Way* (1988) promoted a new way of thinking about the Church's children, based on the 'pilgrim church' model. It suggested that children were on the same journey of faith as adults in the Church[11] and recommended losing the educational image of Sunday schools. Groups became 'Sunday Club' or 'Junior Church' with 'leaders' rather than 'teachers' and a less formal approach. Equally significant, it recognized that the structures of providing training for leaders and teaching programmes had been neglected for some time and that most children left Sunday school at the age of nine years. It affirmed the value of choirs and bell-ringers as well as uniformed organizations as ways in which the Church could engage with children after this age.[12] It recommended research into the spiritual development of children, new liturgies to serve all-age worship, including a form of the Eucharist when children were present, and for parishes to provide realistic finance for resources, training, and personal support for children's leaders.[13]

The later report, *All God's Children?* (1991)[14] was subtitled 'Children's evangelism in crisis'. It questioned whether Sunday was the best day to reach children and affirmed the role of schools as well as other ways in which the Church had hitherto engaged with children beyond the church community. This report received less promotion than *Children in the Way*, with no scheme of implementation. Meanwhile, the world moved on, but the issues highlighted by the report remained.

8.   Children and church today

These various changes have led to a situation where the traditional Sunday school has almost entirely disappeared. Children's nurture is usually held at the same time as the morning service. A few churches have flourishing work in the traditional style, but most churches offer teaching based on the lectionary or other themed resources with the children joining the adults for part of the service. Children are often present at the Eucharist if it is the principal service and, since 1997, have been allowed to receive Holy Communion before confirmation, with the bishop's permission. Most churches will have a monthly all-age service and special services, on occasions like Mothering Sunday and Christmas Eve, that are geared towards children and young families.

Youngsters who attend church on Sunday tend to be the children of the worshipping congregation. In some churches, they are welcomed as equal and valued members of the worshipping community. In others, they are marginalized. Most churches would claim that they try to accommodate children, but, if pressed, many would admit that they have not changed in any significant way in order to do so. This can lead to their children's ministry becoming little more than a 'holding exercise' in the hope that children will eventually become part of the adult congregation. In that mode, nurture is often geared towards entertainment rather than engagement, with little thought of progression or concern for the children's development as whole people. Numbers are often small and recent statistics state that 49 per cent of Church of England churches make no provision for welcoming children to their main Sunday service.[15]

Growing in faith?

A group of children's workers met the new vicar to discuss the development of the small Sunday group. Conversation ranged from discussing the youngsters' involvement in the service to the need for a new teaching programme. The person who organized the children's work suddenly commented, 'We only look after the children. We don't give them anything.'

As we have seen in Chapter 1, extended working hours, dispersed and broken families, with the pressures of a consumerist society leave many families with little time together at weekends. Some parents may want to take their children to church occasionally but it is a small matter on the edge of a crowded schedule. For many more, church services are strange events with no relevance to the life of the average young family. Moreover, today's children are not encouraged to walk more than short distances or travel without adults, so have less opportunity to go to church on their own than was the case in previous generations.

9. The popular picture of today's Church

In one sense, the need to reach out to children who have no contact with the Church today is similar to that of the early days of the Sunday school, before the religious revivals of the nineteenth century. Whatever the benefits (and they are many) of linking children's nurture to the main Sunday service, they have, with the reduction in number of Christian organizations for children and the changed use of Sunday in a fragmented and predominantly secular society, left a huge void in the Church's evangelistic ministry among children.

The overwhelming picture given by the media and, indeed, the churches themselves, is that the most churches see their ministry among children to be something for Sunday morning and nothing to do with the mission of the parish in the wider community. Some organizations, notably Scripture Union, CPAS and BRF, provide resources and help for churches to organize holiday clubs and fun mornings geared towards children who have no other links with the Church. A more common form of outreach is the 'Family Service' with visual aids, drama and lively music providing accessible worship for children and the increasing numbers of adults who had little knowledge of the Christian faith. These have been successful in that some young families, with no other links, are attending church occasionally, but the day and time take no account of the changed use of Sunday in most families.

10. Issues that hinder a ministry among children

If the above description were the complete state of affairs, it would be gloomy. The only paragraph on children in *Mission-shaped Church* focuses on the decreasing number of children attending Sunday school.[16] The source of these statistics does not take into account the other ways in which the Church reaches children that have been discussed earlier in this chapter, although an endnote admits that: 'The actual number of children connecting to church . . . is probably significantly larger than these figures suggest.'[17] While not denying that the situation is serious, such distorted reporting is unhelpful. It is exacerbated in this instance by there being no examples in the original text or in *Mission-shaped Church* of how the situation could be addressed.

The largest obstacle to the Church's engaging with children is a lack of confidence on the part of clergy and children's leaders. This is fed by excluding the ministry with children from discussion and decision-making at both national and local level. These factors isolate and lower the self-worth of the people who are called and committed to working with children on behalf of the Church. It is for the whole Church to make engagement with children and young people part of its mission in the community and to encourage and equip the clergy and leaders who have a ministry among them.[18]

11. Signs of hope

We have come to realize once again that children are spiritual beings, that they have all been on spiritual journeys from birth and that there is more to education than learning facts. We are beginning to recognize the damage that has been done by trivializing religious belief and secularizing our culture. One result of this is that many schools look for advice on the spiritual dimension of education. More clergy are leading worship in school or holding school services in church at Christmas or the end of term. Far fewer parents are refusing permission for their children to attend religious services than a decade ago and relationships between schools and local churches are being restored. This will be discussed in detail in Chapter 8.

In spite of half a century of falling numbers, an increasingly secular society and lack of acknowledgement of the value of children's work by churches, numbers of children worshipping as part of a church are beginning to increase.

According to the 1989 English Church Census, only 14 per cent of children under 15 years of age were in a church-related activity on a typical Sunday and the number was falling.[19] In 2001, seven dioceses recorded an increase in numbers of children and young people attending worship. The increase was significant in five of these dioceses.[20] In 2002, twenty-six dioceses recorded an increase.[21]

In May 2005, the Diocese of Guildford announced that, using figures based on the archdeacon's statistics,[22] their churches had 6,868 children on Sunday registers, but nearly as many (6,615) on weekday registers. As few children attending midweek groups have other links with the church, this indicates that the churches in Guildford diocese are engaging with nearly double the number of children on a regular basis (excluding schools) as would be recorded on Sunday-based statistics. Equally significantly, 25 per cent of the new ways of being church recorded on the Fresh Expressions web site[23] during the first four months (February to June 2005), included children or young people, and 60 of the 350 registered groups are designed specifically for children.

Children and their parents and adult leaders all over the country are being church: often unrecognized, unrecorded and under-resourced. These are signs of the Holy Spirit at work in the world of children and are something to celebrate.

Some of the many ways in which children are being church form the substance of the next chapter.

Some questions for discussion

1. Have we acknowledged that the Church has played a part in the gradual reduction in children's learning about the Christian faith during the last 30 years? Can we learn from those mistakes?

2. Do we resource the children we have at our church, however few, and support their parents and leaders?

3. Are we prepared to change in order to welcome children, or are we prepared to accommodate them only at a time or place that suits us?

4. Are we aware of the importance of grandparents as the vehicle for young children's learning about the Christian faith? Do we support them in recalling their faith stories and bringing their grandchildren to church?

5. Do we have children worshipping God beyond our Sunday worship? Do we support these children and their leaders with our prayers, realistic funding, and by acknowledging them as part of our worshipping community?

3 Children and the Church of today

In the first two chapters, we looked at the society in which children live today and reviewed the varied ways they have been nurtured in the Christian faith. A multifaceted picture emerged, with most children having some kind of Christian education until about 50 years ago. We saw how the changes in culture and lifestyle, with corresponding changes in attitudes to religious teaching and ethos, combined to remove Christian teaching from schools and from daily public life,[1] while the Church, in its turn, often failed to respond robustly to these changes.

Now we move on to look at the many and varied ways in which children have opportunities to experience the Christian faith.

After years of falling numbers and the Church's having lessening contact with children, it seems that the tide is beginning to turn. Numbers are rising as more and more churches find imaginative and varied ways of letting children hear and respond to the Christian story.

1. Where is church: what is church?

In 2003, the Church of England's Statistics for Mission showed a clear increase in the numbers of children attending worship on Sunday. They also showed that the Church was engaging with nearly as many children through 'non-worship' activities, i.e. meetings that might include prayers and Christian teaching, but were not specifically designed as acts of worship.

Simon's Christian life

Simon is eight years old and lives with his mother on a housing estate in north London. He was baptized at the parish church but has no other links with it.

> Simon goes to a Church school in the next parish. Every day
> starts with a Christian act of worship. On Tuesdays, it is led by
> the vicar, who also teaches RE to all the Key Stage 2 classes.
> The children go to church for special services and for some
> history and RE lessons. At the end of each term, they have a
> school Eucharist. Some of the older children and the adults
> receive Holy Communion.
>
> Simon has just joined the Cub Scouts; a sponsored group
> meets every Friday at the Methodist church. Every meeting
> ends with a prayer and the group goes to the parade service
> on Remembrance Sunday and for St George's day.
>
> On alternate weekends, Simon goes to stay with his Dad and
> stepfamily 20 miles away. Sometimes they go to the family
> service at their local church.

This story, which is based on the life of a real child, shows some of the many
ways in which children can have an experience of worship, teaching and
belonging to a Christian community without its being noticed:

- Simon takes part in a Christian act of worship on every weekday in
  term time.

- Simon has Christian RE lessons that include visiting a church building.

- Simon takes part in the sacramental life of the Church through
  school Eucharists and sees some of his friends receiving Holy
  Communion.

- Simon belongs to two Christian communities: school and Cub Scouts.

- Simon may have an opportunity to go camping with the Cub Scouts.
  As it is a Christian group, there will probably be daily prayers and a
  service on Sunday.

- Simon attends worship in three places: his school, the Methodist
  church, and a church near to his father's home.

This leads to the first question, 'Where is church for Simon?' Is it automatically the parish church where he lives, who would not recognize him, or is church for Simon found in one of the many other ways that he is worshipping God within a Christian community? Second, how can one ensure that Simon has the guidance to help him to grow in faith if his various experiences of church are designed solely for youngsters of his age or are occasional visits to a church a long distance from his home?

2.　Children relating to church: a complex pattern

As a substantial number of children come from scattered or divided families, and about a quarter of children attend Church of England primary schools, many youngsters will have similar lifestyles to Simon. Many more will be experiencing worship at other times and places than in church on Sunday morning. It will be through a club or uniformed organization; through school; through occasional special services, or by going to church with a second parent, a grandparent or a friend. Some of these encounters with God will happen in a church building but others will happen in other places and situations.

The picture of how children relate to church is very complex and varied.

a.　Church on Sunday

We have already seen how changes of lifestyle and mobility have eroded the traditional Sunday, but they have also created 'church shopping'. Families will attend the church they like or which offers them the facilities they need. This may involve choosing a church that has several young families and a lively children's ministry. Indeed, many churches of particularly strong traditions will have more people attending who travel a distance than are resident in the parish.

b.　Church away from home life

Some children from divided families may go to a church with their second parent or when they stay with their grandparents, possibly many miles from home. If they attend it frequently, they may make friends there and be welcomed into the children's group.

c. Church schools

As we have seen from Simon's story, many Church schools are distinctive all-age worshipping communities. About half of Anglican schools celebrate the Eucharist regularly and children may be prepared for first Holy Communion, baptism or confirmation. RE lessons are beginning to look towards the spiritual experience in the heart of religion rather than just teaching about different faiths and practices.

The many opportunities for witness and worship provided by schools are discussed in Chapter 8.

d. Midweek groups

An increasing number of children are worshipping at midweek groups. These vary from lunchtime Christian clubs, after-school activities with worship, 'Kidz Klubs', and cell groups, to Saturday morning sessions. They invariably have a higher number of children than will attend that particular church on a Sunday. These activities form the substance of Chapter 5.

e. Toddler groups and buggy services

In many churches, the biggest growth point is with children of less than five years and their parents or carers. The children attending them will be part of a Christian environment and experience worship from an early age. Some of the accompanying adults may use the opportunity to enquire about the Christian faith. This is discussed in Chapter 7.

f. Pilgrimage

There is a revival of the understanding of faith as a journey. With this and the improved facilities provided by cathedrals and other holy places, the number of pilgrimages is rapidly increasing. The whole topic of being a church on the move is discussed in Chapter 9.

3.   Responding to the situation

Having seen the many ways that children can have to engage with the Christian faith beyond Sunday in their parish church, the challenge is for the Church to respond to this complicated and challenging situation.

The principal challenge is for the Church as a whole to own and celebrate the wide diversity and variety in our children's ministry. If this is to happen, it must start by recognizing that there is no second-class worship or 'proper' church. A Eucharist held in the school hall on Friday afternoon is of the same value as one held in the church building on Sunday morning. A group of parents and toddlers praying together during a short act of worship on Tuesday in the village hall is as much 'church' as a small congregation attending Evensong on Sunday evening, and so on. Indeed, it may be more effective as witness in that it meets people where they are in every sense.

This is not negating the importance of the gathered community meeting to worship on the Lord's Day in a building dedicated for that use, but it is seeing the Sunday Eucharist, or other principal service, as the pinnacle of corporate worship, not the entirety. That means respecting and giving equal support to the many different ways in which children are being church, and educating clergy and children's leaders so that they are equipped to respond to the opportunities they present.

This requires a major change of thinking for parishes as well as diocesan staff and Christian organizations that support a ministry among children, and the publishers who provide books and multimedia resources to assist them.

4.   Challenges

It is clear that, for many church communities and, indeed, people in positions of leadership, this owning of the variety of ways in which children are being church requires both a change of thinking about children as part of the Church and a review of the welcome, worship and nurture of its youngest members. On the other hand, once a local church starts to own and take its ministry among children seriously, it will receive a sense of vitality and hope from them.

As there are many opportunities for the Church to reach children beyond the traditional Sunday service, the question has to be asked about why the mission of the Church among children is often overlooked, and invariably under-resourced. Considerable publicity is given to falling numbers of children attending church on Sunday but very little is written about addressing the issues or highlighting the opportunities for growth. This is not only a media issue but is present within the Church: for example evangelism among children is, by and large, the subject taught least to clergy, readers and children's workers.[2]

In 1998, Paul Simmonds, then Mission Adviser for the diocese of Coventry, wrote a paper to examine young people's involvement and engagement with the Church. He concluded: 'Not only are we struggling to keep and care for young people from church families, we are making only negligible impact on the vast majority of young people who are unchurched.'[3] The reference to this paper in *Mission-Shaped Church* maintains that Paul Simmonds and others suggest that 'the Church is primarily set up to minister to the over-40s, at the expense of young people (the phrase "young people" here includes people in their 20s and early 30s, as well as those in their teens).'[4]

This statement can be applied even more strongly to children. Children have no voice and are not able to choose to go to another church or decide how they would like to spend Sunday. If their experience of church at an early age is poor, they will probably vote with their feet as soon as they are able to, towards the end of their primary education. This is borne out by the major dropout rate from church being at about nine years. Similarly, if children's parents are non-religious, the environment mitigates against their having any interest or involvement in religious practice. In *Making Sense of Generation Y*,[5] Graham Cray comments on recent research that supports this statement:

> In addition a recent report of the British Household Survey[6] confirms that parents are the most significant influence on children's attitude to religion, but claims that institutional religion has a 'half-life' of one generation. That 'two non-religious parents successfully pass on their lack of faith' whereas 'two religious parents have roughly a 50-50 chance

of passing on their beliefs.' This research concludes that,
'Younger people most often hold their beliefs as part of a
view of life which they do not even recognise as spiritual.'[7]

5. Obstacles to growth in children's ministry

If the Church of England is truly ministering at the expense of children, what
makes its ministry skew away from them? The answers are many and varied,
but can be summed up under two broad headings: negativity and neglect.

a. Negativity

● Apocalyptic predictions from some Christian agencies, based on
Sunday attendance figures, and the media reporting that follows, both
serve to dishearten children's workers and lower their self-esteem.
This affects their views on the value of the work. They wonder if
there is any point in what they are doing if numbers are only going
to diminish. Some will even give up. Others will feel threatened and
mentally retreat to protect what they have. This destroys imagination
and kills growth. It also negates the value of the midweek ministry
of the Church with children. It can be perceived as second rate and
only of value if it increases the number of children going to the
Sunday service.

● There is a tendency to put the child, and indeed many adults, into a
model of church that is not appropriate. Most worship is designed as
if only adults are ever going to be present, so the expectation is that
children will have to behave like adults, which they are not. Some
people with a ministry among children feel that the recent liturgical
revisions have missed an opportunity to take into account the many
occasions when children are present at the Sunday Eucharist or when
they form the majority of the congregation. The recommendation in
Children in the Way to 'examine the need for new liturgies to serve
all-age worship, and in particular for a form of Eucharist for when
children are present' is yet to be fully realized.[8]

- Some Sunday school leaders will tell Bible stories in a way that says little about the loving relationship between God and his people or about how they should live out their Christian lives in twenty-first century culture. This may stem from the way the adults themselves were taught as children. More significantly, it can show an unwillingness to think through some of the more challenging aspects of the Bible or living out the Christian life and how to communicate them to children. In a recent 'Thought for the Day' on BBC Radio 4, Rabbi Lionel Blue pointed out that children did not want other people's hand-me-downs but their own religious experience. He asked, 'Why should adults dump on children the things that they do not believe themselves?'[9]

- There is a tendency for some adults to place burdens on children that they would not wish to have placed on themselves. This is evident in discussions about children being admitted to Holy Communion, when there is often a desire to expect a commitment from them far beyond that set out in the confirmation service or to demand levels of dedication and behaviour that are not necessarily modelled by adults.

 Carrying burdens

This story was told by a solicitor who specialized in work concerning child protection.

A televised service took place on the seashore. It opened with a penitential rite in which rocks representing sins were placed at the foot of a large wooden cross. Heavy rocks representing the sins of the world, the sins of adults: war, murder, theft, abuse and neglect were lugged across the beach and into place.

Who carried these rocks – these sins, our sins? The children carried them.

The adults stood and watched them.

b. Neglect

- Children can be treated as passive beings, as people to be kept occupied in hope that they may become useful to the Church in the future. This is seen when the criteria for nurture and worship are geared towards containing rather than engaging with fellow disciples and encouraging spiritual growth.

- At present, there is no obligation for clergy, readers or children's leaders to receive education in any aspects of a ministry among children, and its accessibility and content are a matter of chance. In some dioceses, there is no designated person to ensure that any advice or training in children's ministry takes place and there is no scheme of moderation. However, on a more hopeful note, there are now moves to address this at national and local level.[10]

- The number of resources geared towards children's ministry beyond Sunday morning is still very low. There are very few resources for parent and toddler groups, or after-school clubs and yet these are where the Church is growing. There is a huge need for exploration and training in the whole subject of worship with children who have little experience of God.

- As *Mission-shaped Church* states:

  Our commitment to the 'parish' calls us to identify with the totality of those entrusted to us. One third of the population is under 25, but one third of church budgets (or even a tenth of church budgets) is not invested in youth and children's ministry.[11]

  It is not unknown for a parish to have no budget for children's work or for training of leaders.

Double standards: two stories

A diocesan training officer in Yorkshire noted that a church he visited provided beautiful printed weekly service sheets for the adult congregation but the children were colouring pictures from photocopied sheets of very low quality.

A children's leader in a parish in an outer London borough was allowed to keep the collection that the children brought each Sunday to spend on materials. There was no assigned budget.

These issues, and others, combine to dispossess the children and their parents. They negate the value of the ministry of those who work among them. The result is a lack of confidence and sense of worthlessness that is very destructive to children and adults alike.

5. Hallmarks of children being church

Having looked at the ways in which children experience worship and are nurtured in the Christian faith, the challenge is to define these various ways that children are being church. The following list is not exhaustive but will be a starting point:

(a) 'Church' will happen at almost any time and any place.

(b) It will have almost any format (see section 1 above).

(c) It will be incarnational in that it will change in order to engage with children.

(d) It will include worship that has a sense of the presence of God, and helps children develop their own prayer lives.

(e) It will be nurturing: telling the story of God's loving relationship with his people, and ours with each other.

(f)   It will be inclusive in that all will genuinely be welcome. Some groups will be designed for children (with adult leaders), while others will be for the parents and children together.

(g)   It may be geared towards a particular need or interest, rather than serving a geographical neighbourhood.

(h)   It will be transforming, looking towards the future, because it will give each person an opportunity to worship and have a relationship with God. That changes lives.

6.   What of the future?

It is tidier and safer to want to lead everything neatly back to 10 o'clock on Sunday morning. But, just as the pioneers who started Sunday schools to keep children off the streets and teach them to read the Bible never dreamt that this would evangelize the whole nation and be the beginning of universal free education, we cannot know what will happen to the ways in which children are worshipping beyond Sunday morning.

There should be no hidden agenda to use the various ways children are being church as a means of pressurizing them to join the congregation at the traditional Sunday service. Apart from respecting each group's integrity, we have to accept that this objective is unlikely to be successful. It is a case of the various ways of being church coexisting within the church structure, rather than one competing with the others. The traditional services remain but the church has several congregations. The challenge is to hold them together.

In Luke's account of the shoal of fishes (Luke 5.4-9), Jesus orders his disciples to cast out into the deep, to do something new and risky. They answer with a protest, 'We have worked all night and caught nothing', but the result is such a great harvest that they need help in landing it.

Children are being church in new and risky ways. There is the potential for a huge harvest if we, and that is the whole Church, not just those in leadership, recognize the potential and work with what is there now, rather than looking for an ideal situation. As with any new project, however, there is always an element of risk. Whatever is organized and planned before the event, (and those elements are vital), there are always a number of unknown factors and an element of surprise.

While we focus on forcing our children into a single model of church, numbers will continue to fall however we may work at it and vary it. This is not how life is today. A multifaceted outlook brings opportunities and hope for the future.

Some questions for discussion

1.   Do we already have children's activities that could be considered ways of being church that we have not recognized?

2.   Look at the hallmarks of children being church, in section 5. Which of these values characterize the children's activities under review?

3.   Which of the various ways of being church identified in this chapter would best serve the needs of the children and young families in your local community?

4.   Are we prepared to 'launch out into the deep', to do something new and risky to enable children to hear and respond to the gospel?

4 Feeders, not food: shaping the traditional church for children

The previous chapter identified ways in which children were meeting to worship, including meetings and activities that took place at times and places other than Sunday morning in the church building. It briefly explored the theological perspective of the many ways that children, and sometimes their families, were being church.

The rest of this book explores the many different ways in which children are meeting to worship, learn about and express their faith. In this chapter, we review how churches can engage with children from the basis of their present services and activities. This is not an exercise in nostalgia, but about revisiting the things the traditional church does already and regaining some of the confidence we have lost in our ministry among children. We have the tools for engaging with children and need to find the best ways to use them in today's cultural climate.

1. Ministry among children in the inherited church

Contrary to popular opinion, children do go to church on Sunday, and, in spite of falling numbers, and the increased ways that children are being church on other days and in other places, over half the youngsters who have contact with a church worship there on Sunday. Other children attend occasional services and visit the church building. These present enormous opportunities for local churches to engage with children who have chosen to come to them.

Since the publication of *Children in the Way*[1] and other reports, there has been a rediscovery of the Church as the pilgrim people of God, journeying together. As with any journey, 'At times, the children and adults will walk along together. At times, the children will lag behind and some of the adults will have to wait for them or urge them on. At other times, the children will dash ahead'.[2] As we have seen in Chapter 2, this resulted in the establishment of informal nurture taking place at the same time as the main Sunday service in most churches, with the children being present in church for part of the time. This has been only a qualified success in that, in some cases, little attempt has been made to accommodate children and young people in church.

At its best, however, children are welcomed as part of an all-age Christian family. They experience the beauty of holiness in buildings designed for the glory of God with music, stained glass and furnishings to give a sense of the numinous. Some children are actively involved in leading worship Sunday by Sunday as choristers, servers and bell-ringers. Even more take part in special services by reading, leading prayers, helping with sidespersons' duties and displaying their artwork. Every child can be caught up in the sense of the presence of God and be part of the worship of his people.

2. Feeders, not food

It is often said that faith is caught, not taught. Children can be led to worship God through experiencing the treasures of the liturgy in a traditional setting. Spiritual growth comes, however, through teaching and learning as well as experience.

The introduction to this book reflects on the tendency to treat children as passive beings: children who are expected to sit quietly and be good; potential Christians to be contained until they are grown up and can contribute financially and practically as part of the church structure. This does not necessarily imply neglect (although that is not infrequent) but a lack of awareness of their status as baptized Christians and the importance of resourcing a ministry among them.

Every congregation needs to ask three questions that have a bearing on each church's attitude to children:

1. Do we subconsciously treat children like fish, commodities to fill the pews (rather like food in a freezer) and thereby ensure the Church's future?

2. Is our ministry with children one of containing them[3] (like fish in a keepnet) in the hope that they will be of use at some time in the

future, or is it one of engagement with and encouragement to grow in love and service of God?

3.   Do we encourage our children to be feeders, that is, to grow spiritually, by accompanying them through the difficult times of their faith journeys, when they are questioning and challenging matters of lifestyle, faith and even their own identities? Indeed, do we see these issues as difficulties or signs of growth to be welcomed and encouraged?

3.   Sunday worship that includes children

Children go to church on Sunday, but numbers are often small. This will be for a variety of reasons. We have discussed the social and economic ones in Chapter 1, but these remain only part of the answer. There are other issues: accessibility and resourcing, as well as the style of nurture and worship.

For some parishes, addressing these issues may involve making a few minor alterations; for others it may require a paradigm shift. This is an enormous subject, but can be summed up under three key words: welcome, quality and depth.

Welcome

Welcoming children is more than smiling at them and using their names, though, with children who attend regularly, that is essential. It is about recognizing children as fellow Christians and ministers of Christ with something to give to the Church as well as to receive. This has implications for everything that a church does.

The Sunday worship is for the entire Christian family. It is not a case of allowing *them* (the children) to come in to *our* service, but of two parts of the congregation coming together after their own nurture, or ministry of the word. Taken to its logical conclusion, this means that when the family of God gathers around the altar it is incomplete unless the children are present. It also means seeing that the church building is accessible to children by having a ramp and space for buggies, low chairs where appropriate, and the needs of children being included when discussing any changes to buildings.

Quality

Is the service carefully planned and well executed? Worship with children is one of the most difficult services to lead but is often given to the person with least experience and training. It is essential that people who lead family services be trained in both designing and leading such worship. This includes advice on preaching and teaching that is appropriate for a congregation of a wide range of age and spiritual growth.

Is the children's work well resourced, with leaders who have experience of working with children, and are given opportunities to receive appropriate training? Is their meeting place, however simple, clean and warm?

Depth

Do we give the children a sense of the presence of God in our worship with music, colour, light and silence? Do we encourage them to pray in their own words and in the silence of their hearts? Are their questions respected and time given if they want to talk through their hopes and fears?

Children deserve to receive the riches of the gospel and to be aware of the depths of God's love for each one of us. There is a tendency for services with children present to be geared towards the superficial and the quick joke, sometimes at the expense of a child. There is a place for humour in worship but, as we can see in the ministries of Christian clowns, the humour and the tricks always contain a deep and searching message.

4.   Family services

Many churches have a family service on one Sunday of the month. They reach people who would not come to church every week but will make an effort to be there once a month. They reach the fringe; they reach young families. They will follow one of three formats: eucharistic worship, a Service of the Word, an informal service either based on published material[4] or designed by the clergy or lay leaders. They are difficult services to lead, especially if they have no prescribed format, as they will be engaging with a congregation of all ages and stages of faith, including adult enquirers and children who attend church only occasionally. The General Synod report on training in ministry among children, *Children Included*, highlights the need for tuition in this specialized subject to be made widely available.[5]

Whatever the design, the overarching aim is to give people a sense of the presence of God, and to allow them to give and receive at their own level.

5.   All-age Eucharists

For churches where eucharistic worship is the norm, the monthly family service may be a Eucharist that is designed with children in mind. This may include the presiding minister giving a brief commentary on the sections of the service, having just the Gospel reading, simplified prayers, maybe led or composed by the children, an interactive sermon and music that is straightforward and easy to sing.

The following story of a children's choir in the predominantly retired congregation at Winchelsea in East Sussex is a typical example of a group of children taking a leading role in the worship. They have not only added a new dimension to the parish liturgy, but the parents and siblings who come to support them have added two more generations to the gathered community.

 ### Evangelism through music

Winchelsea is Britain's smallest town. One of the Cinque Ports, it is situated on the south coast of England, near Rye, in a beautiful conservation area. It has a population of just 400 people. Most of the residents are retired professional people. A Church school caters for the local children and those from the surrounding villages.

All that remains of the huge medieval church, dedicated to St Thomas of Canterbury, is the sanctuary and crossing. The congregation numbers about 40 and included only a few children until Marion, a musical Pied Piper, formed a children's choir. On the last Sunday of each month, the congregation is almost doubled when the children's choir takes charge of most of the Eucharist. Fifteen children, dressed in white sweatshirts with the church logo, lead the music, read the Scripture readings and provide the intercessions.

The congregation is supportive of the choir and keen to raise its profile in the community. The annual service of the Cinque Ports was held in Winchelsea in 2005, with the Lord Warden and the local dignitaries and Sea Cadets present. The children's choir was involved with the music and seated in prominent places.

The youngsters come from neighbouring villages so they are dependent on their parents' goodwill to get to rehearsals and services. Most of them attend the Aided school, where Marion teaches music once a week.

The choir has grown because of evangelism by the children themselves. They enjoy it and bring their friends along. Their parents and younger siblings come to support them, and so have added two generations to the congregation.

Two of the children have been confirmed and some other parents have inquired about it. The rector sees their attending the services as part of the choir as evidence of their commitment. He describes the children's choir as an integral part of parish life.

The issue of children receiving Holy Communion is beyond the scope of this book, but whatever the policy of a particular church, every child should always be welcomed for a blessing. In churches where children are admitted to Holy Communion, the sight of them receiving the sacrament alongside adults who receive a blessing is a powerful reminder that our faith journeys are not geared to chronological age and that God's grace is given freely to everyone, regardless of age.

Where eucharistic worship each week is the norm, but this sort of all-age celebration is seen to be impracticable, some children are celebrating the Eucharist together in a simple version adapted for their needs. Eucharistic worship in Church schools will probably incorporate most of the features of an all-age Eucharist. The subject of worship in school is discussed in Chapter 8.

Children are making Eucharist as part of a children's club; they are meeting on Sunday morning for a liturgy designed for them; they are celebrating it at camps and on pilgrimages. The two things they have in common are that the congregation will be almost entirely children, and that they are not necessarily part of a traditional church. Some youngsters will be on the edge of faith and from non-church backgrounds.

story
story
story
story

The God-Bods

Higham is a village of 4,000 in north Kent, between two rivers and the towns of Gravesend and Rochester. The parish church, St John's, held one regular Sunday service, a Sung Eucharist at 9.30 a.m. It also had a legacy of a lively and inclusive monthly all-age Eucharist dating from 1988, which drew large numbers of young children.

Most of the children go to the local primary school, but transfer to a variety of secondary schools, each several miles away. One issue was that, when children left the primary school, they often lost contact with their friends from church and, given the pressures of social life, sporting events and homework, attending a service at 9.30 on a Sunday morning was not realistic. The answer was 'God-Bods'.

God-Bods is open to any child who worships at St John's, from his or her last term in primary school. It starts at 6.30 p.m. with a simple Eucharist that lasts from 20 to 30 minutes. Each youngster is given a task as he or she arrives: to read, serve and so on. Prayers and teaching are straightforward and

geared to the youngsters' lifestyles and needs. The programme
continues with food and either activities or an outing: bowling
and ice-skating are popular. Some youngsters are prepared for
confirmation as part of the ongoing programme.

6.   Special services

Children come to special services and they bring their parents. These
include Christingles, Christmas carol and crib services, and celebrations
on Mothering Sunday and Harvest Thanksgiving. Members of uniformed
organizations may attend church for a parade service on Remembrance
Sunday and at St George's tide. These are often the best attended services
of the year and wonderful opportunities for outreach.

A service geared towards children also gives the possibility of new contacts
with organizations and groups who are not frequently involved with the
church. Clergy or lay leaders can arrange to visit the group a few weeks
before the service and talk through the content of the prayers, and
encourage the youngsters to write their own or lead them. This allows
the leader to talk through the children's joys and sorrows as well as the
current issues and news.

Similarly, an imaginative use of the subject of the service can involve children
while presenting a strong teaching point. Children can carry crib figures at
the correct moments in the Christmas narrative and build the crib. They
can take part in a question and answer session with a roving microphone,
and do simple crafts such as making their own palm cross, as part of
the worship.

Christingle disco

St Mary's Swanley is in a town on the edge of the M25. It has a mixed community but the parish church is situated between the shopping centre and an area of some deprivation.

Each year it holds a Christingle service at 5 p.m. on the last day of the school term and follows it with a disco, so it is an end of term service as well as a Christmas party. Over 200 youngsters usually attend the service. They present their Smartie tubes filled with coins for the Children's Society, and collect their Christingles. The disco is lively and food is plentiful. The parish regards the event as part of its outreach to the children in the community as well as the first of its Christmas festivities.

7.   Occasional offices

Children come to baptisms, weddings and, occasionally, funerals. This may be the first time they will have entered a church and, although some of them will have travelled a distance, at least a few will be local children visiting their parish church. The service will be part of a deeply emotional event, the promise of a newborn baby, the excitement that accompanies a wedding, and the sorrow and confusion of what may be a child's first experience of death.

The children have come because they want to celebrate something special in their families, including the life of a special person, yet the service can be a deeply excluding experience: a strange building with a strange ceremony in unfamiliar language. It is vital for clergy to be inclusive in their speaking and in naming the children if close family are named in the prayers. It is equally important to offer the same welcome and facilities as would be on hand on Sunday mornings. The youngsters may even return or go to another church near their homes, if the service was a good experience that makes them feel positive about the Church.

The village wedding

Ash church is a medieval building with minimal facilities, but as it is part of a housing development, there are a large number of weddings, which invariably include young children.

As part of the welcome before the arrival of the bride (as well as the usual notices about confetti and collections), the rector, John Peal, says that the policy is that nobody takes children out of Ash church. If they make a noise, he speaks louder! Then he indicates that toys and books are available, and invites the children to use them.

This simple notice has the effect of relaxing the parents, ensuring that the children are welcomed as members of the gathering on a par with the adults and providing for their needs should they become restless. It does not prevent children being taken out of church, but sends a positive message about encouraging them to remain for the service and feel at home.

At baptisms, children can be invited to stand near to the font so they can see what is happening. The *Common Worship* baptism service has very rich language, so a brief commentary in everyday words helps the children to understand the actions. It would probably be appreciated by the adults as well! A few resources are listed in the section on further reading at the end of this book.

Similarly, funerals can be confusing for children and it is helpful to offer the same support and resources as for baptisms and weddings, as well as reminding children and adults alike that this is a time for saying 'Goodbye' to and 'Thank you' for the person who has died.

8.   Visitors and pilgrims

Many children visit church buildings as part of their life at school. They come for RE and history lessons and may use the building for a school service, a concert, or a play. Some children visit churches as tourists when they are on holiday. The challenge here is to make it clear that this is more than an empty and possibly ancient building, but the place where a living community meets to worship God.

For many children, entering a church building will be their first contact with church, and may be the only one they will ever have. An old and empty building with bare seats and pointed windows can frighten some children, and even adults can feel ill at ease. A warm church with music playing quietly gives a feeling of welcome and helps the children to relax. A few spotlights on the altar, pulpit and any pictures or icons emphasize which parts of the church are important. A prayer board and, if it is your tradition, candles, show that the church is a place where people come to pray. Time to explore the building and enjoy its atmosphere is part of enjoying the sense of the presence of God.

For some clergy, it is rare to have a captive audience of anything between 40 and 400, but that is exactly what is offered when a class with teachers and helpers visits a church for a lesson or the whole school presents a Christmas play or holds an end of year service. This is another wonderful gift and worth taking a lot of trouble over. A few members of the congregation could make it their ministry to welcome and support visits.

On a practical note, a school visit will have an educational focus, so the clergy or people who are showing the children the church should have a meeting with the teacher to discuss the learning objectives. It is important to stress that the church visit is about experiencing a place of worship, rather than just teaching facts. The children can learn the facts at school and then bring them to life when they see them in the context of a church.

9.   Accessibility

Having discussed the basic principles raised by the three key words (see p. 43), and the opportunities for engagement through the traditional worship of the Church, there are still questions of accessibility and small numbers.

However high the quality and genuine the welcome, Sunday worship is still held at a time and in a place that is inaccessible and strange for many people.

Children are the most affected by this. However fascinated they may have been by a church building, however much they have enjoyed the services they have attended, they do not have the independence to go to church when their parents want to do something else. Moreover, in many cases they cannot go to the church without an adult because they are too young or it is not within walking distance. A few churches will organize a 'walking bus' or arrange for children to travel with another family but, whatever is organized, children's attendance at church is dependent on the goodwill of their parents. It follows that any outreach among children has to include the whole family.

Most of these issues can be addressed by having a second service. If the practice of church attendance being reserved for Sunday remains strong, this could be by having a service on a Sunday afternoon or evening. A Church Army parish evangelist, based in Belfast, addressed the need for an alternative to a traditional service by organizing parallel worship in the church hall within the framework of a parent and toddler group.

Praise & Play on Sunday morning[6]

Richard wrote:

Sadly, it's not often you hear small children badgering their parents to go to church! Yet this has been a regular cry from some of the children who attend St Matthew's Sunday service for parents and toddlers in the Shankhill area of Belfast, called 'Praise & Play'.

We have now been running a year. The ingredients of the service are hinted at in the name – there is play, using a hall that resembles a toddler morning, refreshments, crafts and a service of worship that lasts about 25 minutes. We don't do 'late', which is very important with young families! It is all very child focused with plenty of lively songs and actions.

'Praise & Play' marks the start of a journey for both children and parents. We have received support from about twelve families, a third of these coming weekly. Only one family would have been regular at St Matthew's before. For parents, it is the start of a faith-based link with the life of the church. We are beginning to build a sense of family and have just started a number of Sunday discussions with opportunities for the adults to explore their faith a bit deeper.

About 35 people attend Praise & Play each Sunday. As it moves into its second year, the challenge will be to sustain a service that nurtures the children as they come to school age while retaining the aspects that are geared towards welcoming families with babies and toddlers.

The following story shows how the idea of holding a monthly service at the parish hall has gradually transformed the worship of the whole community.

The Church went to the children[7]

Fawkham and Hartley are two villages in north Kent, each with its ancient church. A road divides the two parishes and, for a thousand years, it was a farming community of about 150 people.

After the First World War, houses, shops and a parish hall were built along the lane and Hartley gradually expanded with new housing and a school. The churches were remote from the population. A Sunday school met in the parish hall. The parents dropped the children off, drove to church, and collected them nearly two hours later. In 1993, the PCC decided that, as the children could not get to church, the church would go to the children by having a monthly family service in the hall.

The services flourished. A few years later, the PCC decided to hold the main service there every week. The monthly family service would remain, and there would be a Eucharist with children's activities during the Ministry of the Word on the other Sundays. Care was taken to maintain a service in both church buildings each Sunday, Holy Communion in one and evening prayer at the other.

Today, over a hundred people attend the service in the hall each Sunday, too many to fit in either of the ancient churches. New families come because they know that the worship is appropriate for their youngsters. People without cars can walk there, and elderly people enjoy the company of young families. It is warm, there are loos, and coffee afterwards! The most recent development was to rename the hall the Church Centre, because that is what it is: the Church in the centre of the community.

A summary of the ways in which children and their parents are being church away from Sunday and the church building forms the subject of the next chapter.

Some questions for discussion

1. Do we genuinely welcome children as fellow disciples with much to give as well as to receive?

2. Is there a way in which we could offer more or adapt our present services in order to engage with children, while maintaining our traditions?

3. Are our special services seen as opportunities for mission and of as high quality as the main Sunday service?

4. Do we offer the same facilities and inclusiveness at occasional offices as we do for other services?

5. Have we given thought to the effect that our church building can have on children who may never have visited a church before? Do we regard it as part of our mission in the community?

6. Is the church building the best place for all our services? Would another venue serve different people?

5 Cast out into the deep: new and risky ways of being church

In Luke's account of the shoal of fishes, described in the Introduction to this book, the fishermen have worked all night and caught nothing. Jesus tells them to go fishing again and Simon protests: it is a waste of time, but if Jesus insists, he will do it. Jesus orders the fishermen to go into deep water, a risky area full of danger. The result, as we know, is a catch beyond their wildest dreams.

This chapter will explore some of the ways the Church has 'cast out into the deep' by reaching out to children where they are, that is, beyond the Sunday morning and special services in church. Although these initiatives are sometimes described as 'new ways of being church', some have, in fact, been operating for years, but they have either been considered a minor part of the Church's service in the community, or have hardly been noticed at all.

1. What is meant by 'church' for children?

A statement of the Church of England's mission purpose is, 'The Church of England exists to be a Church for the nation.'[1] This has enormous potential, but it can tend to lead the Church to think of itself as being equally accessible to everyone. It is strengthened by the traditional picture postcard image of an English village with a church building literally in the centre, usually accompanied by a green and a duck-pond. The natural way to draw this would be as a series of circles with a building in the centre.

This model, however, has two major flaws.

First, it marginalizes some of the Church's most effective worship and outreach among children. A packed Christingle service, a parent and toddler group, or children singing carols in an old people's home are easily dismissed as 'fringe activities' with a corresponding lack of respect or resources. They can be seen as a means for getting children to come to church on Sunday, rather than valued as equivalent forms of worship and witness among young people and their families, that is, 'church'.

Second, it suggests that it is possible to reach the so-called fringe that is equidistant from this centre and drag its members in or let them sit on the boundaries. This is a false premise because the church is not in the centre of the community or of most people's lives, and has not been so since well before today's children and their parents were born. Church, if it matters at all, is a small factor at the edge of a crowded life alongside school, sport, computers, hobbies, friends and second families.

2.   'Being church': defining the indefinable

The term 'being church' has become popular currency, but is difficult to define. The use of the term reflects a desire to see the Church as the people of God, and a reaction against the common and still widely held view that 'church' means a dedicated building, and that, ideally, worship should take place in one. The use of the term 'church' may also conjure up images of a group of people who meet regularly at the same time and place. This was the assumption when a young mother asked to speak to the rector after attending a buggy service. 'We would like to have the baby baptized,' she said, 'but the problem is that I don't go to church.'

He replied, 'What have you just been doing then?'

What is 'church' for you?

Rosie Tallowin, a families' worker in Essex, found that in any of her thinking about the Church she automatically included children. She accepted, however, that this would not be everyone's response. It would be an enormous leap for some committed and devout Christians to accept that some groups for children and their families were worshipping Christian communities, or 'church'. She wrote:

I have been rereading bits of *Mission-shaped Church* to get my mind back into what it is saying for children's workers in our capacity of being a voice for the children. I realized, when rereading it, that I had automatically included the children, but that this is the way that I see church.

For example: midweek church. At our church, we have two midweek services. One is not what many people would recognize as church or a service, but the other is.

On Tuesday mornings, people of all ages gather together in the presence of God; usually we sing, pray, have a reading from the Bible, a talk, etc.

On Wednesday mornings, adults gather in the presence of God. They don't sing, but they pray, have a Bible reading, a talk and then they take Holy Communion.

What are the differences? We currently have about 80 people on a Tuesday morning, some with children and some without, mostly non-churched, who want to be there, but most of them don't know why, or who is responsible for drawing them there. In holiday times, our group continues to run and we recently had over one hundred people as families brought their school-age siblings.

> The midweek Communion Service on Wednesday has fewer
> than ten people.
>
> For me, midweek church is Tuesday – and I read Mission-
> shaped Church in that way, but I can see now that if midweek
> church for you is going to Holy Communion on Wednesday,
> it creates a very different picture of what it is to be church.

We say, 'Come to church' but many children, sometimes with their parents, are already worshipping together, or 'being church', but we do not recognize it. For most of them, attending a traditional church service would involve a long journey, literally and culturally, into unfamiliar territory: a strange ceremony in an alien building. This being the case, it raises the question whether 'being church' with its image of buildings and an institution with unfamiliar customs is a helpful term for describing a group of children meeting and worshipping together. Perhaps 'Christian community' is a more appropriate term in some cases.

For the purposes of this book, the term 'being church' is used to describe a group of children, with or without their families, who meet and worship together. It counteracts any tendencies to diminish the value and status of worship taking place outside the church building. It is also used when children are witnessing through the way that they live and the things that they do in their schools, localities and with their friends, that is, having a 'ministry on Monday.' It is gradually being recognized that the appropriate place for some baptisms (and first Holy Communion and confirmation) may be the place where the child's Christian community meets to worship, be it a toddler group, the school or even a midweek club.

The term 'Christian community' is more fluid. It also describes a group of children meeting and worshipping together but this can be less structured, indeed be a group of friends who are bound together by their common faith and enthusiasm. This includes communities of children that are formed for a brief time, for example, at a summer camp, a mission, or travelling together on a day's pilgrimage to the cathedral.

As with any attempt to define the indefinable, neither term is exclusive. The best descriptions are rooted in experience rather than terminology.

Casting out into the deep allows children to be a Christian community (or 'church') wherever they find themselves. Clergy and leaders need to be resourced and trained to recognize and support this kind of ministry among children in all its forms.

3. Common features of new and risky ways of being church

Recent research through the Church of England's children's evangelism initiative, Project Reach,[2] found that there are far more children worshipping and enjoying activities together than had been recorded or celebrated. The low profile of many of these initiatives stems from a variety of sources: lack of confidence on the part of the leaders, not being funded by the parish as part of its work, or a lack of recognition that children's activities beyond Sunday are also congregations, and important parts of the Church.

Raising the profile of these activities has led to more parishes recognizing or starting similar projects, to which children have often responded in large numbers. According to the Church of England's most recently published statistics, for 2003[3], during the month of October, 249,000 children aged between five and ten years attended 'non-worship' activities, i.e. activities that are not services in themselves but may include a short act of worship or a closing prayer. As the average Sunday attendance for children under the age of sixteen years is 164,000, this indicates that churches are reaching a significant number of children through other activities besides Sunday worship. The biggest contact that the Church has with children is, however, through schools. This is the subject of Chapter 8.

Although no two ways in which children are being church are identical, they do have a few common features:

1. Most of them meet at times other than Sunday morning. This is largely a response to the changes in children's lifestyle, discussed in Chapter 1, and the issues of accessibility discussed in Chapter 4.

2.   A large number of groups meet in premises other than the church building. This is partly about accessibility, but also about providing familiar surroundings that are suitable for children.

3.   Group leaders who have told their stories say that nearly all the children who attend their meetings have no other contact with a church.

4.   Some of the children have come to faith since worshipping with the group, and for them this is their church.

5.   Each group relates to a particular network of children. This may be a school or a Christian organization. It may be designed for a particular age group. Groups may also be interest-based: craft, sports, music, drama, etc.

6.   Some groups have an ecumenical basis, either by being a joint venture or through cooperation between denominations in a locality.

4.   Children being church: helping it to happen

Added to this, children are forming their own Christian communities linked by friendships, membership of church-sponsored uniformed organizations, and spending time together on holidays and pilgrimages. They will probably be small groups of children talking, playing or praying together at school or in their homes, but they can lead into growing something bigger.[4]

Any structured activities involving children, however, have to include adults in the organization, decision-making, finance and leadership. A common lament is that there are very few children in a traditional Sunday school. The converse is true with midweek children's activities. Some are so popular that a second group has to be started, while others have waiting lists because there are not enough adult leaders.

All-age cell church in Totton

St Winfrid's, Testwood, in the Totton Team Ministry near Southampton, chose to establish a cell church, based on small groups, alongside its more traditional congregations. Their vision had an all-age dimension from the start, and a number of the cell groups at St Winfrid's were intergenerational.

One consisted of twelve people, aged from three to eighty-two. Five of the members were children aged under thirteen, some of whom came from lone parent families. This group met on Fridays from 6.45 p.m. to 8.15 p.m., because the end of the school week allowed the younger children to stay up a little later. Each week they followed the traditional cell church pattern of 'Welcome, Worship, Word and Witness', and all these were designed to include all ages. In the 'Word' time, the members tried to apply the previous week's church teaching to their own lives, and for this part of the evening there was a 'kids' slot' for the younger members – but for the rest of the evening all were together.

Evangelism and outreach are a central part of the cell church vision. The group began to grow because the children brought their friends along – but the numbers of adults stayed the same. Cell groups are born in order to multiply, but the multiplication of this group was delayed because the adults took longer to grasp the vision of sharing faith and welcoming friends. One of the group said: 'The children showed us how to share our faith naturally and courageously. At first we couldn't keep up; but their example made us keep trying!'

As the previous story illustrates, a ministry with children beyond Sunday can have an enormous effect on a local church. Once the congregation owns this work as an integral part of its witness and service in the community, which contains worship as valid as that on Sunday morning, it gains another dimension. Instead of focusing its resources and interest on a small group of youngsters in one place at one time, it sees the enormous number of opportunities to support church that is already happening, develop a Christian dimension to children's work that already exists, and respond to new opportunities as they arise.

Pressure to encourage and support such a children's ministry may come from within the adult congregation, or it may be an offshoot of the core children's work, for example a holiday club developing into a regular midweek meeting with worship geared towards children. It could also spring from an approach from the community to the church: a group of parents, the local school, a club meeting on church premises that wants explicit Christian input, or another church. However it starts, a clear, shared vision is necessary if the idea is to be sustained. A lot of work with children and young people fails because there is no determined force to keep it on the agenda.

On the other hand, it is vital that the church is aware of changes in its community and responds to them. Some groups will become well established, but others may be short term, lasting for perhaps three or four years. Ending a group should not automatically be seen as a sign of failure but as good stewardship of resources. A new development of small houses will attract an influx of people who are starting families: a 'bulge and buggy community'. Responses to this may include starting a toddler group, baby-sitting rotas, a crèche area in church and so on. In a few years those children will be going to school and the church will need to address a different situation: possibly fewer toddlers but a need for worship and nurture groups on Sunday, contact with the (new) school, establishment of fun days and possibly a holiday club.[5]

5.   Reasons for success

When evaluating these ways of being church, it is reasonable to ask why they appeal to children in a way that the traditional Sunday services do not. It must be more than offering games and fun activities if children are coming to faith and in some cases making Christian commitment through baptism, confirmation or admission to Holy Communion. Similarly, one has to question why a school is able to become a distinctive worshipping community that is church for the staff and parents as well as the children who will rarely darken the doors of their local church building (see Chapter 8, sections 4–6).

On the other hand, a huge amount has been done to bring the child out of the church hall to take part in the main service. There have been attempts to involve children in the traditional Sunday morning service, but the service has usually remained unchanged, with language and teaching designed for highly literate adults. Asking a child to read the epistle, or for a group of children to answer questions about what they have learned, or take part in the Offertory, makes children visible to the adults but it has not actually made the service more accessible to the children. The Church needs to go on affirming and resourcing the children that are at church on Sunday morning and see that they are in the midst of the gathered community.

If the Church is to reach children beyond this, however, it must recognize that confining its ministry to expecting children and their parents to join a gathered and often exclusive community on Sunday in a special building (which is rarely in the midst of the community geographically, socially or culturally) is not enough. Neither is a piece of mission-flavoured tokenism, like holding a single event in the hope that the children will automatically come to church on the next Sunday and become 'hooked', like fish on a line.

The implications of this are huge. It will require a major change of thinking for parishes and every individual or organization that tries to resource its ministry among children. It involves owning and celebrating the wide diversity and variety in our children's ministry and giving it the support it needs. Ways of turning around the way that a church regards its children and building based on what is already there form the basis of the rest of this book.

The following chapters illustrate the diversity of ways in which children are part of Christian communities beyond Sunday morning. Unlike *Mission-shaped Church*, which focuses on fresh expressions of church, this book also explores the many opportunities that the church has to engage with children. It is not an exhaustive list, as one characteristic of the various events is that they evolve to meet a particular group of people in certain circumstances. They fall into three main categories:

1.   Groups and clubs designed for children.

2.   Children together with their parents and other adults.

3.   The school community.

A small and distinctive fourth group, 'the church on the move', consists of some examples that are dictated by particular circumstances.

Questions for discussion

1.   Do we already have contact with children beyond Sunday morning and what more might be done to engage them?

2.   Are we prepared to take risks with our time and finances in order for children to hear the gospel?

3.   Many of the 'kingdom' stories are about the small and insignificant. Are we aware of the ways children can and do support each other and witness among their friends and neighbours?

6 Children's groups as Christian communities

The Church can and does engage with children through a large number of activities, all of which have mission opportunities and some of which could be seen to be Christian communities or 'church'. They are not the prerogative of large and well resourced parishes: some tiny and apparently struggling churches have effective outreach while serving the local community. Some of them develop into being the children's own church; others provide links with families and may lead to their attending special services.

This chapter reviews the large number of different groups and events whereby the local church engages with children. Some of them can appear to be little more than providing childcare and entertainment, yet they are part of the Church's service in the community so they are witnesses in themselves. Providing a cooked breakfast for children or operating a Saturday club while parents are shopping may not be obvious ways of bringing children and their families to faith, but witness often leads to questions, with opportunities for response and evangelism. We can never know what long-term effect a single act can have on the life of a child.

In *The Provocative Church*,[1] Graham Tomlin writes:

> If the Church exists to live and proclaim the Kingdom of God and Lordship of Christ, then everything the Church does can have an evangelistic dimension … [examples]. These things are valuable in their own right … even if they never result in any conversions. However, as they provoke questions they are to become the occasion for proclamation and explanation.

The group leaders must judge the appropriate level of direct Christian input as each situation varies. It may be a short act of worship or a closing prayer. Other meetings and events have worship and teaching and fulfil a similar evangelistic role as that of the early Sunday schools (see Chapter 2, sections 1 and 9). They are where the children meet to worship, that is, their church.

Each section of this and the following chapters provides an outline of the aims and characteristics of a particular children's activity. This is followed by a story and a few comments. As the stories are real situations, they present more than one feature of ways in which children are being church, so it is valuable to look at other references and stories for further information.

1. Fun days and festivals

The simplest and most varied activity is a single event, often called a fun day. Fun days vary from a dozen children meeting for a couple of hours of activities in a local hall or church to a diocesan festival for hundreds of youngsters, in a large school or the cathedral. Some days are for all ages together; others are geared towards children of a specific age group.

The reasons for holding fun days are varied. So are the intended outcomes. For some churches, it will be the first venture into outreach among the children in the community. It does not demand a long-term commitment but, if it is a success, the church can hold another one when it is ready, or offer similar events at half-term or during the school holidays. Some fun days are geared towards the theme of the service on the following Sunday or an approaching festival and may include preparing artwork or music for the service. Other days are free standing with activities and games, with a short time of Christian teaching and worship. Whatever the format, and purpose, the underlying aim is to introduce children to the Christian faith in a relaxed and attractive way, or turn fish into feeders. Indeed, some have been so successful that they have developed into regular meetings and have strengthened the church's other ministries among children.

Simon Marsh, the vicar of Bollington, told the following story. It shows how an activity day reached out to the local children, and has helped to revitalize the entire Church community at a time of difficulty.

Parish power

The story started in 2003. The parish of Bollington in the diocese of Chester was down in the dumps because it had just closed the doors of its old parish church for the last time. A daughter church took on the role of the new parish church and it was there, in St Oswald's, Bollington Cross, that two grandmothers, Jessie and Joan, found themselves wondering how to revitalize the ministry to children. The vicar, Fr Simon Marsh, encouraged child-friendly worship. Two church schools and existing Junior Church leaders were obvious resources, but had enough work on their hands already.

Jessie and Joan realized that it was up to them to do something about re-energizing outreach to children. They thought about holding a holiday club, so they called in Janet Arnold, the diocesan children's evangelist, for advice. Eventually a dozen adult worshippers set about providing craftwork, games, music and Bible stories for a children's activity day.

Two years later, St Oswald's has held a themed children's activity day in every school holiday. They have been held in either of the church schools and twice in St Oswald's itself and are now a regular feature of the church's life. As the group has gained in confidence, it is led without any outside help. Up to 40 children come each time, and after each event have been saying, 'Fab' and 'When is the next day?'

The realization of Jessie's and Joan's dream has done wonders for confidence-building at a rather sad time in the life of the parish. One knock-on effect is that the Junior Church is now flourishing and brings warmth and its own distinctive teaching contribution to the weekly Sunday Eucharist. Bollington is looking forward!

2.   Saturday mornings

Some single events like the above story have developed into holiday clubs or a regular midweek club as the demand has increased and the leaders have gained in confidence.

A number of churches with very few children have replaced the traditional Sunday school with a series of activity days, usually held on Saturday mornings. They include worship, teaching, and activities around the subject with time for refreshments and games. The session can be linked with the next Sunday's theme and provide a link between 'Saturday church' and the main Sunday worship, as well as preparing any children who may attend it.

  Starting from nothing

Underriver is a self-contained village within commuting distance from London. It has 45 children living in the community. In most cases, both parents are at work and many of the children are cared for by au pairs. Most of them travel to private schools and have very full lives.

In 2001, there were no children attending the church. The Sunday school had been closed for ten years. The churchwardens held a meeting with the diocesan children's adviser. They decided that, rather than trying to revive the Sunday school, they would attempt to reach the whole community at a time when the children would be available. After researching the situation, they found that the only possible time was Saturday morning, so they held an activity morning in the village hall on the day before Mothering Sunday, which linked with a special family service.

The wardens still had a list of the name and address of every child in the parish from the recent millennium celebrations, so they were able to send a personalized invitation to each child aged between five and eleven years. Thirty-three children turned up. Activities included parachute games and cooking, as well as colouring cards for their mothers. The children also spent time exploring the church and making banners. Eighteen of them came back with their parents (and the banners) to the Mothering Sunday service.

Three years later, the parish holds a fun morning, which includes some Christian teaching, every quarter. From this a monthly family service has developed and has a congregation, including young families, of up to 70 people.

3. Midweek groups

A growing number of churches are operating some kind of midweek club for children. If they are held every week or more frequently, they need enormous commitment from the leaders and helpers. Not only are the meetings longer than at a Sunday group but they involve giving up a late afternoon or early evening every week during termtime or even for up to 51 weeks each year. This is an enormous undertaking, which needs a well-organized structure, including reserve helpers who can be called upon in case of illness. Most weekly clubs are led by an employed specialist worker or an organization such as the YMCA.

Where this level of commitment is not sustainable, clubs may operate on a fortnightly basis or in groups of sessions for each half term. This is also practical for older children when they have increasing demands of homework, school activities and a varied social life.

There is a wide variety of midweek clubs. Some of them are run as part of a parish's outreach within the community or in response to government initiatives (see Chapter 1, section 9). They provide childcare combined with activities and may or may not include worship and Christian teaching. Most of these clubs are held after school but breakfast clubs are increasing. Other clubs are sessions with games and other activities that include Christian teaching and always have an act of worship.

story
story
story
story

The Lion's Den[3]

Vicky was thirteen and worshipped at St Mark's Wellingborough. She wanted to start a club where children who did not come to church could learn about the Christian faith. She went to a PCC member for advice, but was told that she was too young to run a club on her own, so she nagged each church official in turn until the PCC realized that Vicky not only had a passion for telling the Christian story to other children, she had identified a need. In May 2003, the Lion's Den was founded, the lion being the symbol of St Mark.

The Lion's Den operates on alternate Friday evenings from 7–8.30 p.m. and has about 35 youngsters aged between 7 and 12 years. The leaders are drawn from the congregation and are, for most of the children, the only contact with the rest of the church.

This is church for the children. The evening always contains a circle time and short act of worship. Christian witness and teaching are implicit and is through the forging of caring relationships and the various activities rather than formal teaching. The programme for 2005 included a pancake evening to prepare for Lent, and a Good Friday activity day with worship. The youngsters also made contact with the wider community through a bring-and-buy sale in aid of tsunami victims, and a talk from the local police, as well as an annual outing and barbecue.

4. Kidz Klubs

A distinctive example of overtly Christian clubs is the network of Kidz Klubs. Based on an American model created by Bill Wilson, they can operate anywhere but tend to be centred in urban areas of some deprivation. They are openly evangelistic and are really a lively children's service with the teaching being through competitions and what is commonly called, 'a stunt from the front'. There is a strong emphasis on biblical teaching and the personal love of Jesus for each child. Two members of the leadership team support each child by visiting the family every week. Funding for the clubs may come from local businesses and organizations who wish to support the ethos of the clubs, as well as from Christian charities.

Kidz Klub, Page Moss, Liverpool

Page Moss is an outer estate in the borough of Knowsley, which, according to the 2004 Indices of Deprivation, is the third most deprived borough in the country. Page Moss suffers from all the problems common to such places, yet within this suffering community a new way of being church offers hope.

Kidz Klub meets each Thursday – with a programme for the youngest children at 4 p.m., and the full version at 5.30 p.m. Each lasts for an hour, and includes loud music, raucous songs, messy games, and loads of laughter and hype followed by a time of clear Christian teaching, with a single theme presented in a variety of ways. It aims to be the equivalent of Saturday morning TV, as most of the youngsters who attend have had no previous links with the church. With up to 150 children coming through the doors each week, it seems to be hitting the target.

A key aspect of Kidz Klub is that each child is visited in their home every week, where genuine relationships are developed.

With over 300 children being visited each week, the profile of Kidz Klub throughout the community is high, and our understanding of the realities of life on the estate has grown.

Kidz Klub includes prayer, worship, a collection (all money is given away), teaching, care and support, with mission being intrinsic to all that Kidz Klub stands for. It is not church, as we know it, and is light years away from the usual Sunday school, but for those who come, it is their spiritual home. Increasingly we see whole families coming together, such is the sense of belonging.

Out of Kidz Klub has grown TNT for 11s to 14s, and HEAT (Half Eight at Trinity) for those aged 14 and above – further new ways of being church!

5.   Special interest groups

A significant number of groups are designed for children with a particular interest and have a strong emphasis on education in the subject and personal development. Some operate as open clubs, so the membership is self selecting; others demand a particular level of skill and may only accept a child after an audition. Although their starting points are very different, they are all groups of children held together by the Christian ethos and a common interest.

a.   Uniformed organizations

Uniformed organizations, notably the Boys' and Girls' Brigades, Scouts and Guides, and the Church Lads' and Church Girls' Brigade and their corresponding groups for younger children were founded with a specifically Christian ethos and emphasis on personal and spiritual development. For some children, this is the only opportunity they have to learn about the Christian faith, and see it in practice if they go on a group holiday or summer camp. This is discussed in Chapter 9.

b. Playing together

A church football team or a drama club may be formed because a group of Christian youngsters and a couple of adults who are already in the congregation share a common interest. They may contribute to the social life of the church or link with other churches in the area. Their mission dimension is often overlooked, but they demonstrate to the children's friends that being a Christian includes enjoying normal activities and having fun together. Children are excellent evangelists, so will encourage their like-minded friends to join in the group or team.

c. Ringing and singing

Bell ringers, choirs and music groups exist to give glory to God through assisting with the worship of the Church. As they aim to develop a skill to a high standard of performance, they have a strong mission dimension in that they attract children who are not normally involved in church. The faith is caught rather than taught and the children develop a strong sense of being valued members of the worshipping community.

The following extract from a letter after receiving a grant from the Youth Evangelism Fund shows how a handbell team has added to the musical and evangelistic life of a church in Norfolk.

 Handbells in Snettisham

Thank you so much for the cheque to help improve our handbells that we use on many different occasions with all sorts of people . . .

The bells were used on Friday March 4th in our fundraising 'Variety Show' concert by 26 of my friends. This was brilliant fun and greatly appreciated by the audience of parents and friends from nearby villages and we raised £222.95 for the Tsunami Funds that we sent to MAF and Tearfund . . .

> Our concert theme was 'Jesus the Light of the World' and a
> great opportunity to remind visiting families in the audience
> about the message of our Saviour, the Lord Jesus Christ . . .
>
> We are hoping more Snettisham Scouts and Guides and
> Brownies and their parents will come to our church services,
> especially monthly youth and family ones. They have also asked
> for a 'Come and Try It' bells session as they enjoyed them at
> the youth group's carol service last December. The bells could
> be the way we can include them: some of them already come
> to our Wayfarers and Charisma clubs.

Churches should be aware of the enormous mission dimension of these
various groups, and support them. The story of the children's choir in the
predominantly retired congregation at St Thomas of Canterbury, Winchelsea
in East Sussex (described in Chapter 4, section 5) is another example of a
group of children bringing along their friends to sing, who then bring their
families to the services.

Many adults can trace the beginnings of their Christian commitment to the
teaching at a Brigade or Scout meeting or a summer camp. Football and
drama are ways in which children and adults can spend time together and
youngsters with no other contact with church can see that being a Christian
is very different from the common negative concepts.

There has been a strong link between the Church and music performed
by children (usually boys) for centuries. The experience of being part of
beautiful worship lasts for the rest of their lives. A noticeable proportion
of Anglican clergy's first involvement with church was as a chorister.

Questions for discussion

1. Do we have any children's groups similar to those in this chapter? Do we support and resource them appropriately?

2. Are we aware of the value of our interest-based organizations, both for their ministry as part of the church, and for the strong mission aspect of attracting and investing in non-church children?

3. Has reading this chapter identified any gaps in your ministry among children that should be addressed? Ways of responding are discussed in Chapter 10.

7 All ages together, with children in the centre

Groups designed for children but which also include their parents or carers connect with the community and provide the opportunity to grow a church with two or three generations worshipping together. They allow parents to spend time with their children without the pressures of home and school life and, on a practical level, having parents present solves many of the issues surrounding numbers of leaders.

The assumption that adults *worship* God and children *learn about* him still holds strong in some churches. Groups designed with children at the centre but for all ages to meet and worship together help to break down the traditional model where children's nurture and worship are separate from the rest of the church. They redress the balance and can lead towards the concept of a church that is truly for all ages.

As in the previous chapter, a number of models are discussed and supported by real examples of situations where children and adults are worshipping together as Christian communities, or forms of church.

1. PTO – parents, toddlers and others

As with many of the kingdom stories, the smallest and seemingly most insignificant can become an opportunity for growth. This is the case with the Church's ministry among its youngest members.

The toddler group or preschool is the biggest growth point in many churches and, as well as being a vibrant midweek church in its own right, it can lead to the members becoming involved with other aspects of church through baptism of the youngest children, special services, and then at school. Some parents are enquirers themselves and may hear the gospel message for the first time through discussion at the group.

As mentioned in Chapter 1, many women are delaying having children and find that they miss having interesting careers and the company of colleagues when their first child is born. The result is inevitably loneliness and a loss of confidence as they wrestle with very different skills from those used in their work. It is a great privilege for church leaders to provide friendship and support as they walk beside these people at a time of major change in their life journey.

Squeals on wheels

Great Bardfield is a village in the heart of rural Essex, near to the market town of Dunmow. The agricultural community has all but disappeared, leaving a mixed and transient population, with enough children to support a village school, while their parents commute to work.

When the present priest-in-charge, Robert Beaken, arrived in 2002, he found that there was no Sunday school or similar group. During the vacancy, the reader, a retired teacher, had replaced the traditional sung Eucharist with a monthly family service as an attempt to draw in young families.

It soon became clear that there were three issues to be addressed: to make every Sunday service more inclusive, to encourage wider lay participation and to cater for the needs of very young children and their parents.

As part of welcoming children at all times, the family service and traditional sung Eucharist were drawn into a single service: family Eucharist. A simple musical setting was adopted so that everyone could join in. A carpeted area at the back of the church made a perfect crèche area, with three large toy boxes so that the toddlers and babies could withdraw to play in safety.

The crèche area and toy boxes became the basis for forming a parent and toddler group, Squeals on Wheels. It was evident that the young mothers were very lonely and that the church could give them a place to develop friendships as well as giving their toddlers an experience of Christian worship. Fiona Bretton, the churchwarden's wife, recognized the need and worked hard with Robert to make the group happen.

Sessions are held in blocks of six weeks to coincide with school terms. They are run on Thursday afternoons, ending in time for the mothers to collect their older children from school. Each meeting opens with a simple act of worship, which is usually led by Fiona or one of the congregation, who also help with the refreshments. Then out come the tea and the toys!

About 16 parents with 22 toddlers attend the sessions but, for the Christmas meeting with a mini-nativity play, there was a total of 68 parents and children.

Apart from giving the children and their parents an opportunity to pray and play together, Squeals on Wheels has had a huge impact on the whole congregation. Any fears that they were a church without a mission or a future have completely gone away.

Families are at ease in the church and a few from Squeals on Wheels have started to attend the new family Eucharist. The older children are beginning to play an active role in it, by taking up the Offertory, reading and leading the intercessions. The Christmas carol service was packed and there are plans to offer more services on special occasions.

2.   Buggy services

A buggy service is similar to a toddler group in that it is geared towards very young children and their parents, but it is explicitly designed as an act of worship rather than a playtime that may or may not include worship. Some buggy services may last only about 20 minutes; others may be part of a longer session.

As well as the social aspects that have been described in the previous section, buggy services give children an experience and a pattern of worship from a very early age. They also give parents a chance to worship in a service that is designed with young children in mind, with a relaxed atmosphere. This is church for many young mothers and provides support at a time when attending traditional services may be difficult. It also provides support for enquirers and baptismal families.

Buggy services can be held in the church or the church hall. With goodwill, they could be held at a school, a health centre, or even a house. The design of the service will depend on the age of the children present.

 Barney Bear club at St Barnabas

Preschool children and their parents/carers have been meeting at St Barnabas' Church in Drakes Broughton, Worcestershire, for the Barney Bear club every fortnight on a Thursday afternoon for several years. The session lasts for about an hour and includes a Bible story, songs, prayer, a simple craft activity and refreshments. The church is in a rural, village location and is close to the local first and middle schools. The session is timed so that it finishes in time for parents to pick up older children from school.

In July 2004, when the time came for a group of regular attendees at Barney Bear club to leave in order to go to school, both the children and their parents expressed regret that they would miss their contact with the church and asked if another session could be run for slightly older children, taking place immediately after school finishes. This was accommodated and Barney Bear club continues to meet in the church on a Thursday afternoon twice a month with a further session on a different night once a month for slightly older children. The church is looking forward to growing more Barney Bear clubs, as the children grow older.

It is best to start buggy services by holding them three or four times a year to link with the school term or to introduce festivals such as Christmas, Easter and Harvest Thanksgiving. They can also be held as an occasional addition to a regular toddler group meeting.

3. Family interest groups

The midweek clubs described in the previous chapter for the most part are a combination of three aspects: childcare, games, and Christian teaching and worship. The ethos of the club depends on which aspect is emphasized the most. Clubs designed to provide childcare run without parental involvement, though a few may work as leaders. Some special interest groups such as drama and music may involve two or three generations working together for a production or a service.

In an age when time for parents and children to spend time together away from the demands of home and school is increasingly limited (see Chapter 1, sections 1, 2 and 6), a group that allows them to enjoy a hobby or interest while worshipping and exploring their faith together is an invaluable form of church, that may become more popular as the need arises.

Care has to be taken, however, that children of working parents are not excluded. This can be through forming a network of parents who will look after a second child and take him or her to and from the group. Although the presence of parents lessens the number of leaders needed, child protection procedures need to be followed very strictly for the protection of all concerned.

**story
story
story
story**   **Messy Church in Cowplain**

Lucy Moore, a member of BRF's Barnabas Ministry
team, started Messy Church at her parish near
Portsmouth. On one Wednesday each month, children and
their parents come straight from school to spend time
together doing an hour's craft activity. Any children whose
parents cannot attend the meetings are accompanied by
another adult, either a relation or the parent of another child.
This is followed by a short service in church that relates to
the activity. Then the families return to the hall where they are
given a high tea.

Lucy included the meal because she felt that the difficulty with
family activities in the late afternoon was that parents had to
rush home to feed hungry children immediately afterwards.
She also felt that eating together encouraged fellowship. She
chose to base the meetings on a craft activity but it could be
music, drama, games or any other activity. They have had up to
a hundred people at a meeting but after a few months, the
numbers have settled to about seventy people.

4. Family activity days

A family activity day is similar to the above event or a 'fun day' but is more
explicitly based on a biblical teaching or the Church's year. Adults and
children work together on a particular project as part of the preparation
for the following Sunday or the approaching season.

The most popular theme and time is Holy Week, with a Good Friday activity
day that focuses on the Cross and Passion while looking forward towards
Easter. Activities may include making hot cross buns while teaching about
their symbolic ingredients, creating the Easter garden, making cards and
practising singing 'Alleluia!' They can start or finish by joining a procession
of witness in the local area.

Other days are largely craft based: baking bread for Holy Communion, organizing displays for Harvest Thanksgiving, making an Advent wreath or banners or an altar frontal. They can also be geared to drama, as the following story demonstrates.

Scratch nativity in Devon

As most of the churches in the diocese of Exeter serve rural areas and have tiny congregations, many children do not get a chance to take part in a nativity play.

Since 2001, children in Exeter diocese, with the help of adults, have rehearsed and performed a nativity from scratch in an afternoon. People arrive at a large church at 2.30 p.m. and make themselves comfortable. For the best part of 90 minutes, songs are learned, dance steps practised, and even a heavenly host of paper angels is made. The main characters are chosen and costumes adjusted to fit.

Then comes a well-earned breather! Cakes, biscuits and drinks are eagerly devoured and then it is back to starting positions for the performance. Parents and friends gather to see the result of an afternoon well spent. The musicians give the singers their cue and the well-loved story of Mary and Joseph's journey to Bethlehem and the events that followed unfold. Animals dance in the stable; a camel train weaves its way around the building; angels sway in the sky; and the magic is worked again.

Of course, none of this could happen without a well-organized group behind the scenes, but it is exciting and encouraging to produce and perform a play with music from scratch. In addition, the new songs and actions learned can be taken home to be performed in the children's own churches at Christmas.

The sense of achievement and the look on the children's faces is an example to everyone!

Some questions for discussion

1. Do we have any groups for children with their parents or carers similar to those in this chapter? Do we support and resource them appropriately?

2. Do we address the needs of the adults as well as the children in our groups? As we teach and worship with the children, are we aware that some of their parents may be hearing the gospel for the first time? Are we prepared to walk alongside them as they question and explore the Christian story?

3. Has reading this chapter identified any gaps in your ministry among children that should be addressed? Ways of responding are discussed in Chapter 10.

8 School: an all-age Christian community

Mission-shaped Church recognizes that 'the network based around the school . . . is a key grouping that may be receptive to the gospel'.[1] It suggests that this can be encouraged by sharing of services in school or after school. The section on school-based worship expands on this slightly, but stresses the value of the school building as a meeting place, with opportunities for parents to worship alongside their children. It does not mention the children's own spiritual development and contribution. Even this is, however, only a small part of the picture. A good Church school will be a Christian beacon in the community where the children are encouraged to grow in faith and live by Christian principles. All that it is and does is grounded in worship, with children, staff, and some parents and governors taking part. Indeed, some worshippers would describe it as their church.

This chapter attempts to present a broader and more accurate picture of the role of schools as part of the Church's mission in the community. It specifically looks at the Church school as an all-age worshipping community with children playing a vital ministry. First, however, it explores the valuable relationships that can be forged between a church and all its local schools.

1. Schools exist for children

If a person is asked where children are to be found, the automatic answer is usually 'in school'. Schools exist to educate children, their buildings are designed for children, and they are probably the only place in the community where large numbers of children gather. It is sometimes forgotten that they are also all-age communities composed of people of all ages and backgrounds. A primary school in an inner city area may have students who speak 30 different languages and who come from a variety of social and religious backgrounds. A secondary school in a small town may have the students' own parents teaching them, cooking the lunches, or maintaining the building. Many adults are part of a school community: parents, teaching and support staff, governors, voluntary helpers, clergy and community leaders, all of whom have an interest in the school, and in some instances may spend more time in the building than the children do.

2.   Part of the 'cure of souls'

Every school is situated in a parish. That is a significant statement in that it makes each school as much a part of a 'cure of souls' as any other group of people who work or live within the parish boundaries. The local school is in the centre of the community. Parents and carers gather there daily. The hall is used for meetings, evening classes, uniformed organizations and even parties. In some communities, it may be the only sizeable meeting place.

During the last ten years, there has been a new openness to children experiencing worship and taking part in religious activities. The spiritual dimension of a community school is examined by OFSTED; so are the RE and collective worship.

Contact with any school is dependent on the goodwill of the headteacher and governors but an increasing number of schools welcome links with the local faith communities. This presents enormous opportunities for churches to witness in a way that has not been possible for about 40 years. Some headteachers, however, do not wish to work with a church, and this should be respected.

The subject of school groups visiting and using church buildings for services and other events has already been discussed in Chapter 4 (section 7), but there are many other opportunities for churches to reach out to local schools.

Many rural churches feel beaten by having scattered congregations and small numbers. The following story shows how, with imagination and cooperation, a great deal can be achieved.

Celebrating together in a rural benefice

Two people from a remote team of six small parishes, Lifton, Broadwoodwidger, Stowford, Lewtrenchard, with Thrushelton and Kelly with Bradstone, near the Cornish border, were so inspired by a diocesan training day on building relationships with schools that they invited the diocesan children's work adviser, Rona Orme, to speak to their team council to 'enthuse the troops'. She spent an evening in a packed village hall discussing ways of engaging with children beyond Sunday.

Six weeks later, the two enthusiasts had approached the four schools in their benefice, of which two were Church schools, to invite them to join in a big harvest celebration, which would include a focus on the needs of children who live in areas of famine. They thought about booking the Methodist church, which could provide an arena-style hall. This approach involved the Methodist minister in the planning and leadership.

Three of the schools joined in with enthusiasm. Each school prepared a twenty-minute musical or dramatic presentation on a different aspect of harvest, coordinated by the churches. One looked at the wonder of creation, another celebrated harvest bounty, and the third considered the inequalities of food and poverty across the world. Each school included prayers that the children had written.

The event eventually took place in the new function room at Roadford Reservoir, with panoramic views over the lake – a wonderful backdrop for a harvest celebration.

Hopes that they could raise funding for a professional music group to work with each school were not realized, but the event was a quality experience for the children that met many of the requirements of the national curriculum as well as being an act of worship that drew the schools and churches together.

The two organizers, one of whom was a parish children's leader, visited each school afterwards with a gift of biscuits for the teachers.

There are now plans for a holiday club next summer, run cooperatively between the parishes, the Methodist circuit and the schools.

3.   Opportunities for witness

Evangelism is about witnessing by presence and the way that we live out our Christian lives as much as about teaching and faith sharing. People who attend a church tend to want to support a Church school. They might be of more service in a community school, where they could be the only Christian voice. Christian families with children in community or private schools provide a valuable ministry and Christian witness in all sorts of ways.

As well as engagement through worship, RE, and visits to the church, there are numerous opportunities for witness through Christian people being involved in a school as paid staff or volunteers. Members of congregations can be involved as governors, helping with reading or in the classroom, assisting with administration, and supervising children on school visits or during the lunch hour.

Helping in a classroom or taking a reading group may not seem to be particularly Christian tasks, but being 'Christ in the playground' is as valuable a part of witness as more overt teaching. As we have already discussed at the beginning of Chapter 6, such service may not produce obvious results but we never know the effect that the smallest action may have on the life of a child. Indeed, a church member serving as a governor, employee or volunteer may be the only Christian voice in the school community, to ask questions about the funding for RE, collective worship, or policies to do with the ethos of the school. Further ways that Christians can be involved in the life of a local school will be developed in *Mission-shaped youth*, to be published by Church House Publishing in autumn 2006.

 Two stories: Witnessing through service

Rose was a midday meals supervisor in a primary school. She told how some of the children had seen her going to church on Sunday and realized that she was a practising Christian. When it was raining, Rose had to take the children into a classroom and keep them occupied. 'I tell them stories,' she said. 'Sometimes they are stories about Jesus. The children keep asking for more!'

Phil, a curate in a dockside parish, found that he was regarded with suspicion by his local primary school, whose intake was predominately Muslim, but his offer to help with football coaching was accepted. Kicking a ball with the youngsters gradually built up relationships and trust so that he was eventually welcomed as part of the community and able to give pastoral support and then invited to lead some of the school's acts of worship.

4.   School-based worship

Schools are not just places for children to be educated. The local primary school is often a centre for the whole community and may be physically as well as psychologically more accessible. Holding a short service designed for parents and children may attract elderly people as well because it is easier to reach and has better amenities than an ancient church building. Some churches have moved a weekday Eucharist to the school so that the congregation worships with the children.

Attending worship in school may also provide an incentive for adults to enter an unfamiliar church building, in that people who have become comfortable and relaxed when taking part may eventually become willing to make the extra journey to a school service in church. The following story shows how a project flourished, stopped, and was then recreated in a different way.

story
story
story
story

Church into school and back again

In the late 1990s, the vicar of Sutton-at Hone and Horton Kirby in the Darenth valley near Dartford wanted to encourage more young families to attend church. Holding a monthly midweek service at Sutton-at-Hone church had not been successful, so he moved it to the school to see if that would draw more people.

Even though the school and church were situated in the same road, the difference was striking. The first week, there were 14 people. After a couple of services, they were bowled over by the interest, with helpers having to put out extra chairs as people arrived. After six months, there was a regular congregation of 55, mostly, but not entirely, parents and children.

The service continued for some time and then gradually stopped as fewer people attended it. The vicar retired in 2003.

However, the seed had been sown. His successor, Fran Papantoniou, arrived a year later and restarted an after-school service in the school, which is very well attended by staff, pupils and parents. The latest development is to hold termly services in the church. Parents are invited to them and she describes them as, 'always packed out'.

In the neighbouring school of Horton Kirby, the children come to church for prize-giving each year. A close practical link is formed each Sunday by the children's group, of over 30 children, meeting in the school and then coming into church to join the rest of the congregation for a blessing at Communion.

Other examples of school-based worship can be found in *Mission-shaped Church*.[2] They are markedly different, however, because they look at the opportunities provided by the building and network of several generations, but do not take account of the many Church schools that are worshipping communities.

5.   Church schools, praying communities

The Dearing report, *The Way Ahead*, describes Church schools as, 'at the centre of the church's mission'.[3] Elsewhere it reminds the reader that it has:

> some 900,000 young people attending its schools . . .
> Our experience is that the vast majority give their pupils
> the experience of the meaning of faith and of what it is to
> work and play in a community that seeks to live its beliefs
> and values.[4]

Schools live this out in differing ways. The increased interest in the practice of religion has also freed schools to be more overt in proclaiming their specific Christian ethos and education. Many schools have prayer corners or worship areas in their classrooms, and the practice of having a prayer board where the children can write petitions is growing. About half of Church schools celebrate the Eucharist, and staff and children alike may be baptized and admitted to Holy Communion at school. This was unknown ten years ago and has had a transforming effect on the community.

Children's own experience of worship and the Christian environment of a Church school may lead them to evangelizing their own families and friends. We cannot overestimate the evangelistic ministries of children among their families and friends.

The assistant head of St Edward's RC, CE, VA Secondary School in Poole, Dorset, Heather Waldsax, described it as:

> a Christian school which is very aware of the world we
> live in and there are members of staff who are able to put
> together reflections and acts of worship to respond to events
> at short notice. Resources of prayers and reflections have

been built up over the years with this in mind. We believe that it is important to be aware of the spiritual needs of our students and staff in relation to what is happening around us, and to respond to them.

This is lived out through the school's worship, but also the relationships between the staff and students, the pastoral care, and the service in the community. The following case study is a small but telling example of the respect in which the members of the community hold each other and the place of prayer in their corporate life.

Praying together

When the Iraq war broke out in 2003, many of the students at St Edward's secondary school, Poole, felt that they wanted to do something to express their concerns about the destruction and inevitable loss of life. The staff understood the frustration that the young people were feeling and decided that that their feelings should be respected. Two senior members of staff took time to plan during one morning.

At midday on Wednesday 19 March, a majority of students and staff participated in a 15-minute voluntary peace vigil on the grassy bank outside the school buildings. A focal point was provided by some Year 9 students who removed their blazers and spelt out the word 'PEACE' with the whiteness of their shirts. In addition to prayers for peace, prayers were said for the families of all those involved in the current conflict.

For the whole of the week, the chaplaincy team planned for the chapel to be a focus for students to reflect and pray for the world situation. There was always someone present at break and lunchtimes if students wanted to talk, as well as being encouraged to be quiet and pray.

6.   Distinctive all-age eucharistic communities

Some Church schools have become the centre for worship for not only the students and staff but also their families. Parents will come regularly to join in the worship.

For many youngsters and, indeed, adults, the school's daily worship is 'church' for them and the school should be recognized and respected as a worshipping community. This includes holding major services, including eucharistic worship, baptisms and confirmations, in school as well as church, and ensuring that all school worship is of a high standard and priority.

Being church at school[5]

The mission statement of Christ Church Primary School at St Leonards-on-Sea is 'Learning to live; living to learn – I have come that you shall have life'. For the 480 pupils and several dozen adults, this distinctive eucharistic community in the centre of a UPA of deprivation is church.

The life of the school is based on prayer, the core being the twice-termly Eucharist. The liturgy has developed over the years; it is the children's own service. They write the prayers, plan drama and readings, lead, and sometimes compose the music. Any KS2 child who wishes to be prepared to receive Holy Communion will join an ongoing nurture programme with a member of staff being a sponsor and prayer partner.

Collective worship opens with a candle being lit and everyone singing 'Jesus, you are the light'. Class worship is held in the classroom's worship space, which is designed by the children. Some of them sit beneath a decorated hanging mobile.

The school's intake is multi-ethnic: 28 languages are spoken. Many youngsters come from deprived homes, or are fostered, or in care. There is very little bullying and suspensions are rare. The ethos is to be Christ to one another. Young students are given a 'buddy': an older child to help with any problems. This may include praying together or writing on the prayer board. Issues are talked out in circle time and resolved together.

The children recognize the school as a safe place where each person is valued. Some past pupils will return to the school to discuss difficulties. Many will choose to forego a half-day's holiday to come to the end of year Eucharist. Large numbers of parents also attend it, and will turn to the staff and clergy at times of need.

School worship, like the above example, can turn on its head any preconceived ideas about the children not being suitable to take part in eucharistic worship or that a service geared towards children is somehow inferior. A school Eucharist can be truly an all-age service, with some children being communicants and some adults being blessed. Difficult students and harassed staff may find reconciliation when they share the Peace. Teachers may be eucharistic ministers and children will lead the prayers. The vicar may take a back seat and contribute only to the parts of the service when a priest is needed.

7.   Evangelism in school

We have reviewed the opportunities for witness and teaching through almost any local school, and the way that a Church school can be a way of living out the Christian life.

Children may come to faith because of what they have learned at school. A vicar found the parents of a child in the Church school on his doorstep one evening. They opened the conversation by saying, 'We decided that we would allow our children to make up their own minds about religion. Our daughter has just told us that, from what she has learned at school, she wants to be baptized. What do we do now?'

Not only the students come to faith through experiencing church in school. Some parents who attend worship at their children's school have a background of a Church school education or have been involved with a church when children. Taking part in an act of worship in a familiar building and a relaxed atmosphere leads some of them to revisit their faith and ask questions. In 2000, a school on a housing estate ran an *Emmaus*[6] course for a group of such parents.

Developing a relationship with any school requires sensitivity and patience. Schools that welcome Christians in an official capacity or as visitors do so in a spirit of trust. A badly prepared act of worship, inappropriate teaching or a clumsy approach can set back years of good work and will not be forgotten. It is an abuse of that trust if contact with the children is used to attempt to proselytize or to invite them to a particular church. A Christian presence in school is a witness in itself and will lead to questions and opportunities for discussion with the staff and parents. Working with children in school is a great privilege and responsibility as well as presenting enormous opportunities.

The role of the specialist schools' worker is described in Chapter 10.

Some questions for discussion

1. Do we have a school in our parish?

2. What contact do we have with our school already? This will include staff and parents in the congregation and members of the church community knowing children, possibly as neighbours, who attend the school.

3. Are there ways in which we can develop contacts with our local school?[7]

4. Have we seen Church schools as part of the Church's mission in the community?

5. How is the local Church school an all-age church? Are there ways in which this could be celebrated or developed?

9 The Church on the move

We have reviewed some of the ways that children's groups operate at a distance from the church building: in schools, village halls, and community centres. Children are also witnessing in their daily lives, in school, meeting in people's houses and the open air, or going on pilgrimage or to a camp to spend time together and draw closer to God.

This chapter describes a series of situations where children are forming Christian communities away from a fixed building. Each example is distinct and has an aspect of responding to God in a particular way.

1. Witnessing to their faith

In the chapter on schools, we have discussed how adult Christians can witness to their faith as employees or volunteers in schools. This is not necessarily by explicit teaching or leading worship. Children and adults alike may learn far more about what it is to be a Christian by these people's presence, service and behaviour towards each other than from the best formal teaching.

Children also witness to their faith by the way they behave to each other and the principles by which they live. The story, 'Being church at school', (see Chapter 8) describes the school's ethos as 'to be Christ to one another' and records how bullying among youngsters from diverse and disadvantaged backgrounds is almost unknown.

The conscience of the village

Two girls nearing the end of their time at primary school were deeply affected by the project, 'Operation Christian Child', so they organized a collection for it. This led to their becoming aware of the many other needs of the world: environmental issues, famine, disability and sickness, to name but a few. As they gained confidence, they started to ask their neighbours for sponsorship and offered to do chores to raise money for a charity. They support a different charity each fortnight and research the subject thoroughly.

The community overwhelmingly supports the youngsters. One resident admitted that they had made her uncomfortable by their commitment to doing what they could to make the world a better place, and described them as, 'the conscience of the village.'

This story and many other examples demonstrate the difficulties of seeking to define terms such as 'church'. Such stories are, however, one of many ways in which children (maybe unconsciously) are providing examples of Christian living in the community. In an age when both children and the Church are the subjects of negative media reporting, it is important to record and celebrate the way many children live out and witness to their Christian faith.

2. Pilgrimages and Christian holidays

Recent television programmes on cathedrals, monasteries and the religious life reflect a new interest in holy places, and the whole subject of pilgrimage has suddenly become popular. Cathedrals and shrines are being recognized again as places of spiritual significance as well as historic buildings, with people of all ages, including children, going on pilgrimage to their local cathedral or further afield.

Some cathedrals have family fun days and festivals for children. A single family can join in or the children can go as a group. Most diocesan Boards of Education organize festivals for the local schools and parishes. They serve to remind the children that the Church is bigger than their own group or congregation and that there are more Christian children than they had realized.

Some churches or Christian organizations run Christian camps and holidays each summer. Young people go on pilgrimage to Taizé, Iona, and Walsingham. For a few days, a diverse group of children becomes 'church', a Christian community with the time spent making friends, and the fun rooted in prayer and Christian teaching. For some youngsters, the time spent in the company of other Christians plays a significant part in their coming to faith, marked spiritual growth, or taking a step of commitment. The section on uniformed organizations (see Chapter 6) recorded how many an adult can look back and recognize the influence that a camp or other holiday had on their Christian formation.

 Pilgrimage: a journey into faith

Every spring, over two hundred youngsters, some familiar with church, some not, from all across Britain arrive in the middle of the Norfolk countryside, at the Shrine of Our Lady of Walsingham. They spend the weekend engaged in unusual and specifically age-targeted worship, prayer, workshops and fun. Then they go home again!

Does this have any missionary value? Is it offering a real experience of 'church', is there any way such an experience can awaken 'faith' in these children? Valid questions are posed by many.

Pilgrimage is essentially about journeying. There is the sheer physical effort involved in making the journey to a holy place. Arriving at the site of pilgrimage is itself the start of another journey of discovery. For children it is no different and, when they embark on the children's pilgrimage weekend, they are thrown in at the deep end. They learn by hearing the words of Scripture through acting, dance and dramatic readings. They focus on the message of Walsingham: the Incarnation brought about by one woman's 'yes' to God, and they hear repeatedly how Jesus loves and values each one of them.

The children are drawn into prayer by use of music, dance, drama, visual and tactile stimuli, and silence. They are encouraged to think and receive without any expectation that they should respond in any particular way. Lighting a candle, receiving water from the holy well, praying through colour paint prayers, or waving flags and ribbons are about the child's relationship with God.

As with any pilgrimage experience, they are able to step outside their everyday routine for a short while and enjoy this unique space, so, inevitably they think about their lives and the lives of others back home.

This is a very real experience of 'church' and evangelism in action. At the end of it, they are going back into their normal daily routine. It is not an attempt to take them away from this; the return home is as important as the pilgrimage itself – the journey called 'life' continues.

Drawing on her experience as the education officer at Walsingham, Janet Marshall reflected on the evangelistic focus of a pilgrimage and whether it can be instrumental in helping children on their faith journey.

We know from the many verbal and written responses from children of all ages that they feel and think differently after they have taken part in the children's pilgrimage. Many are already asking far-reaching questions about what the world of faith means in their own lives. Many want to know how they can continue to 'do these sorts of thing' at church back home.

Some youngsters may wish to 'draw a line under it'. We meet young adults, however, often years later, who have come back to their faith journeys. They remember how, years earlier, a pilgrimage or school trip to Walsingham kindled a fire. Now they are ready to take another step and recommence the journey.

3. Children's housegroups and cell groups

Housegroups for children, whether a small self-contained group or established on the cell church principle, are becoming better known. As with most forms of 'new' church, they have been happening for several decades. Children's housegroups based on the cell principle were operating on Wednesday evenings in South London as part of the Baptist Church's outreach in the community over 50 years ago!

The informality and friendliness of a living room lends itself to welcoming youngsters who may be daunted by a church or hall, and encourages discussion in a relaxed atmosphere. It provides an environment where children feel valued and able to invite their friends. It must not be forgotten, however, that extra care has to be taken with both child protection and health and safety issues in a private house. Rigorous standards must be applied for the protection of the leaders as well as the children, including setting boundaries for the times that the group meets.

ExCELLent

ExCELLent is a midweek cell group for children aged 7 to 13 years based at St Luke's, Colchester. The leader is Claire Johnson.
Its aims are:

- To provide an opportunity for ongoing discipleship in a small group, enabling the children to deepen their relationship with God.

- To provide a group to which the children feel they belong and of which they have ownership.

- To enable the children to discover and develop their gifts by encouraging them to take responsibility for leading parts of the programme.

- To provide an environment where they can invite their friends.

The group meets on Thursday evenings from 6 to 7.15 p.m. and operates on three weeks out of every four during term time. Three weeks follow the cell programme:

Welcome: an icebreaker activity and a snack.
Worship: using CDs, or in more creative ways, such as writing creation poems.
Word: Bible teaching and application to help them move on in their journey of faith.
Witness/works: a response to the Word, in either prayer or a practical way.

The fourth week is Kidz Klub, providing an opportunity to invite friends to a fun event. There are four zones:
Chill out: funky seats, tuck-shop and live DJ.
Challenge: prizes for top scores in crazy challenges.
Creative: crafts.
Games: play stations, table tennis, football and dance mats.

Each session ends with everyone together for a messy game and a short Bible-based teaching slot.

Over the last year, our vision has changed and is changing. The group has started to develop a life of its own as a worshipping community, becoming a fresh expression of church. During the last year, we have had a Passover and a Christingle. Through our midweek programme, both church and community children are in regular contact with the church: building relationships, coming to a place of learning, worshipping and praying; a place of nurture and discipleship, equipping and empowering.

4. Church without walls

A problem raised when trying to connect the Church with the community is that the church building is inaccessible. This is not a recent phenomenon. In the Middle Ages, the Black Death or decline in local industry caused people to move away and the village became derelict while the church building remained. In the last century, cart tracks have developed into dual carriageways, separating the parishioners from their church. Housing built on the edge of a village is often some distance from the church building. Churches have responded to the challenges in a variety of ways, but, as with every other situation, the children have been affected the most as they are dependent on adults to provide the means for getting them to church, wherever it is held.

Some large housing developments or new towns, for example, Milton Keynes, include church buildings from the beginning. Others use the school or community centre for worship. This has the advantage of teaching children (and adults) that church is the people of God, rather than a building where people go to worship.

Children at Grange Park Church

Grange Park is a new estate of 1,800 houses in Northamptonshire, the oldest being five years old. There are children everywhere, with an oversubscribed primary school. Most people are not local but have moved to be in the London commuter belt. The minister's wife, Charlotte Nobbs, describes it:

The Church is a group of people who worship together. We meet for corporate worship in the local community centre, and less formally in people's homes, walking in the woods, sharing communion, playing rounders in the park, or over a barbecue. On Sunday, there are as many children in church as adults; we use every available bit of space, whether the foyer, the playing field, or going for walks as part of the service. We encourage children to grow as disciples of Jesus and to reach out to others, so the focus is not on Bible stories week after week, although they are taught regularly, but on building friendships, and having fun.

The children enjoy socials and parties and, at least once a term, they make party invitations, invite their friends along to a party during the adult church when we play games including 'Simon says' turned into 'Jesus says', a fun, interactive Bible story and huge amounts of party food. We have nativity and Easter puppet shows, telling the stories of Jesus using nursery rhymes, well-known songs, interaction, and food and craft activities.

In the summer the church sets up gazebos on the green outside the school for mornings to run Kidszone for three mornings, providing refreshments, face painting, a toddler and baby zone, arts and crafts, bouncy castles, games and a prayer zone. It is free, because God's love is free, and it attracts about 600 people. The older children work with the adults to make this event successful.

We run a monthly midweek group, Stepping Stones, to tell Bible stories to preschoolers and their carers, using song, nursery rhymes, shakers, props and puppets, ending with a craft activity to remind the child of the story, and a short time of prayer before breaking for coffee, cakes and play. Some of these parents have joined an evening group (Stepping Stones Plus) to explore what it is to know Jesus.

Throughout the year, we work with the health visitor to run a new mums and babies group from my home. This is a safe place for them to recover and make friends, build community, and find help to combat postnatal depression and isolation.

Having or not having a church building is not an issue. The church is freed up in many ways and able to think creatively, because many of the stifling constraints of an old, historic building are not there. We focus on being part of the community of Grange Park; to go out to the people rather than imagine they might like to come to us. We contribute to anything good that goes on in the community, whether it is community fireworks or helping at the school fete, and see our input as blessing what Jesus is already doing in Grange Park.

Questions for discussion

1. Do we recognize the ways in which our children are being Christian witnesses in the community? Do we acknowledge the courage that this takes?

2. Have we been on a pilgrimage or had a parish day or holiday? If we have, is this something that is truly inclusive?

3. Do we help children to feel they are part of a larger Church through attending events, working with other local churches, or supporting the work of mission agencies?

4. What can we learn from the distinctive forms of church at ExCELLent and Grange Park?

10 Methodology: Moving towards a child-shaped Church

This chapter offers some practicalities behind children being part of a mission-shaped Church. We have reviewed the various ways in which the Church is engaging with children, through its traditions and liturgies, its schools and the variety of events and activities that are mission opportunities. We have also noticed the enormous contribution to proclaiming the gospel that children can make through their own worship and witness. The discussion points at the end of each chapter really ask one question: does anything in this chapter ring a bell for you and your church? Do you have something like this happening already, or does it give you a pointer for a way in which your church can include children as part of its mission in the community?

Having answered 'maybe', or even 'yes', the next move is to see how a congregation can move forward to celebrate what is happening already, to improve where necessary, and to encourage initiatives that help children to hear the gospel message and become Christian communities, or 'church' wherever they find themselves.

1. Recognizing church in all its forms

One of the biggest challenges in developing any children's ministry involves persuading the church community to accept that this is the responsibility of the whole Church. However simple the plans are, the church community needs to be fully informed and own the project, even if individuals disagree with it or do not want to be personally involved. A common obstacle to evangelistic work among children is that its success is measured only by the numbers of children in church on Sunday.

Exciting schemes are often not implemented because they have not been thought through. Many an imaginative idea has never been realized because a zealous PCC had hedged it with obstacles and choked the life out of it. 'Casting out into the deep' means going into unknown situations. The vision, however, has to be underpinned by planning and resources if the Church is to respond effectively to the ministries of its children and those who are beyond the immediate Christian family. This applies as much to a single event, or developing a relationship with a school or an existing group, as to setting up a new project.

A single book can only give an outline and a few examples of the ways in which children can be part of the Church's missionary life. It is important for clergy, members of PCCs, and children's workers to seek advice before making any detailed plans. There is a list of organizations and further reading at the end of this book.

2. Giving children a voice

It must be stressed that, whereas a group of adults can create their own ways of being church, children are almost entirely at the mercy of the goodwill of their families and the PCC. Children do not have access to finance or meeting places, and as we have already noted, in most cases they are not free to roam beyond the confines of their homes and schools without their parents (see Chapter 1, sections 3, 6 and 11). It is vital that children's voices are heard and their needs are wholeheartedly supported. The story of the Lion's Den is a case in point (see Chapter 6, section 3). Vicky recognized a need to reach out to the children in the locality but, as she was a child, her vision depended on her persuading someone on the church council to raise the subject on her behalf at a meeting.

Listen to the children

A major Christian charity recently asked for its work to be reviewed by a team of independent assessors. This included its educational material. Experts had regarded it highly and it had even won awards. This particular assessment included asking for the views of the children who had used it. It was found that the children overwhelmingly dismissed it as dull, irrelevant and with low visual impact.

This has led to a major re-thinking and structuring of all the materials for schools and children's churches.

3. Context

In *Mission-shaped Church*, the chapter on methodologies states clearly that the context should shape the church, and that this should be the template for any development.[1] Chapter 2 of this book showed how the Sunday school movement was founded to respond to a social and educational need. It also described how the Church has failed to take account of the changes in children's lives and culture, with a devastating effect on the numbers of children attending Sunday school or services, but how other forms of church are reaching large numbers of youngsters.

It would be very easy to look at a particular example or story and see if resources are available to replicate it. This would almost certainly be unsuccessful, as it is taking a pattern out of context and expecting the children to fit into it, like fish caught in a net. The following aspects need to be looked at by any church that wants to take up any of these ideas. It is advisable to address them in the following order to obtain a complete pattern:

a. Sunday worship: how do children find the church services?

As over half the children with some links with a church attend worship on Sunday, it is sensible to start by reviewing the worship that takes place in the church building on Sunday. An interesting exercise is to ask adults for their earliest memories of church. Answers will include memories of not being able to see and the long sermons, but also, hopefully, feelings of being welcome, and enjoyment of the beauty and the action. Any review must include children, however, for their experience is not necessarily the same as the adults' memories. Asking a group of children what they like and dislike about church may bring different answers and be thought provoking. Whatever they are, they should be heeded and addressed.

One children's worker occasionally uses graffiti sheets at the end of a service called 'Service with a Smile☺' to ask children and adults such questions as:

- Today I learned:

- Today I liked:

- The best bit today was:

- Please can you change:

- Please can you include:

- At Service with a Smile☺ I really like:

Adults help non-readers record their views, which are sometimes in pictures, and the planning group uses the comments as part of its regular review.

The whole subject of involving children in the main Sunday service is huge, but the basic premise has to be that the service welcomes all to worship, whatever their age or status. This often requires a paradigm shift on the part of some of the congregation and sensitive handling of the liturgy and those in leadership roles.

A practical exercise that involves everyone is to make a video recording of a Sunday service, including shots from different parts of the church and some from the level of a child who is seated in a pew. It will almost certainly be found that any changes that need to take place for the sake of the children will be welcomed by adults as well.

Special services geared towards children and their parents are inevitably well attended. Before producing more of the same kind of service, however, review what makes them successful. This may include the time and the day, the venue and the publicity as much as the content.

b. What ministry with children is already happening?

Start by thinking about the local schools. Review the present contacts and the relationship between the parish and its schools. Does the congregation pray regularly for the schools, pupils and staff? Has the church invited the headteacher to speak about the work of the school, for example, on Education Sunday? Are there ways in which the church and school can serve each other more effectively? List the resources the church has to offer in people, skills, use of the church building and any needs that the schools may have. Then list the assets the school may be able to offer the church. Arrange to meet the headteacher and go forward from there. Be prepared to listen and learn: be where the school is, not where you think it should be.

A common response to the question, 'Do you have a children's ministry?' is 'yes' if there is a Sunday school or similar group and 'no' if there is not, even if there is a strong ministry with the school. In *Not Just Sunday*,[2] a simple chart shows thirteen examples of ways in which children are meeting and worshipping together, excluding church services and school. Review all the children's activities that are happening and see how each one should be resourced and celebrated.

Make a list of all your contacts with children, including information about each group, however small and apparently insignificant. Take time to research them, including finding out how long they have been running and whether they have particular needs. It may be that a group is struggling because of small numbers and lack of leaders. It may also be because the group is growing rapidly and needs more leaders, funds, or space. The story of the cell church in Totton is an example of this sort of issue.[3] Addressing issues may include major decisions like suspending a group or service that is failing, combining forces with another church, seeking further funding or new premises.

c. Where are the social needs of children in the community?

The review of the present ministry can then be extended. This will be by researching any gaps in the provision for children in the locality as well as the church and school. For example, a PCC worked on a similar exercise in a parish that wanted to develop its outreach in the community. It discovered that there was a Brownie pack and a ballet school for girls but no uniformed organizations or comparable interest groups for boys.

An obvious need in an area with a large number of very young families would be for some sort of toddler group, buggy service or group for new parents. Before starting such a group, check with health professionals if there is a need and whether there are already plans to address it. You may be welcomed with open arms, or you may find that a group is about to open elsewhere. Cooperation rather than competition is an important part of any development.

d. For whom is the envisaged group intended?

This is not exactly the same as identifying a gap in provision but is concerned with the circumstances of children and their families. In starting Messy Church, Lucy Moore identified three characteristics of the young families in her parish: an interest in craft (as many of the children had artistic parents), parents and children who wanted to enjoy time together, and the need for a high tea – the rest of the family presumably eating much later in the evening (see Chapter 7, section 3).

A group may be intended exclusively for children with a particular interest. This may spring from a group of children, maybe from the same school who enjoy football, or children joining with an established adult group to produce a parish pantomime. It could be equally dependent on having an enthusiastic adult at the right place at the right time. The founding and success of the children's choir at Winchelsea, for example, was due to the talent and enthusiasm of one person, who was then supported by the parish (see Chapter 4, section 5).

Accessibility is of equal importance, especially in rural and some inner city areas where few people have cars or children rely on adults to escort them. A school, a room in a community centre or a private house may be a better option than a church or church hall.

e. How will it be organized?

Organization is about sensible planning. This involves knowing the underlying aims, identifying suitable leaders and basic resources such as a place to meet, a programme and funding.

If these first steps are not planned properly, the project will be disorganized, with false starts as the leaders try to correct mistakes as they go. Meanwhile the children will be dissatisfied and, if their needs are not recognized, they will get a negative picture of the church and spend their time elsewhere.

A checklist for any group will include:

a.   Having the permission and prayerful support of the PCC.

b.   Following child protection and safety guidelines.

c.   Ensuring adequate funding for the group.

d.   Seeing that the premises are safe, warm and pleasant.

e.   Ensuring that leaders are competent and appropriately trained.

f.   Having a list of adults who will deputize in case of illness or emergency.

g.   Keeping parents fully informed.

h.   Providing pastoral support by visiting families, especially at times of need.

i.   Being aware of and ready for any impending changes, for example a group becoming too big, key people moving house, new families in the area.

Some of the resources on children being church, and on evangelism, listed at the end of this book, will expand on this subject. It should also be included in any good club programme material.

One maxim should always be remembered: start with something small and manageable that operates within your limits, then let it grow slowly. Rosie Tallowin's flourishing Tuesday church was originally a group of six mothers meeting in someone's house and grew slowly from there (see Chapter 5, section 2). It is better to have a waiting list than to create burnout among leaders, and a large number of disappointed children.

f. Will it be geared towards children on the 'fringe' or children with no experience of the Christian faith?

These two groups loosely correspond to the 'de-churched' and non-churched' groups described in *Mission-shaped Church*, but the former will have had some Christian experience rather than having belonged to and then left a church. The word 'church' is deliberately avoided in this section because of its connotations with attending worship in a particular building. The difference here is about some knowledge, and maybe experience, of the nature of God (by any name) and in particular as revealed in the Christian faith.

Children on the fringe will have some basic knowledge of God and the life, death and resurrection of Jesus Christ. They will have had first-hand experience of worship, either through school or by going to occasional special services at church. Children with no experience of the Christian faith may lack the basic concept of 'God', his works and the possibility of a relationship with him. The word 'Jesus' may be thought to be an expletive rather than the name of a person, and not connected with a picture of a baby on a Christmas card, let alone a worldwide religion.

Whatever they may claim, most programmes for midweek and holiday clubs assume that children are on the fringe of faith, and the teaching is on the lines of developing this knowledge and coming to some sort of commitment. Unfortunately, the subject of experiencing a relationship with God through worship and prayer is often sidelined and teaching is taken at a fast pace. Whatever its strengths (and many are excellent) a programme is hardly helpful if, after three days, a child says, 'Excuse me. Who is Jesus?'

With children with no experience of the Christian faith, one has to start a lot further back and expect to build a community in the group and explore ways of living and issues that interest children before introducing any spiritual aspect. This is long-term work and is under-resourced, but the writing of Mary Stone,[4] the lecturer and former headteacher, and some aspects of Godly Play could be helpful; so would using a 'circle time' similar to that used in school.

Whatever the composition of the group, it is safest to assume no knowledge and be prepared to progress faster if the children are found to have some experience of the Christian faith. Asking questions or making assumptions can make children with no knowledge feel they are failures with the obvious results.

4.   Leadership issues

Leadership of any children's group is always an issue. It requires commitment, expertise, stamina and patience. Apart from any other reasons, this is a very good argument for not holding a children's group (except those with a high childcare component) on a weekly basis. Some people who are unable to be committed on Sunday may be interested in helping with a group that meets less frequently at another time.

It is strongly advised that such a leader will have considerable experience and have received appropriate training. This includes having a mature faith and an awareness of how children learn and develop spiritually. Every diocese should provide training either in-house or through Christian organizations. The outcomes of *Children Included*,[5] the General Synod report on training for a ministry that includes children, include ensuring that such training is available to all clergy and lay people who require it. Local authorities and colleges also provide excellent basic training for a nominal sum or free of charge. Uniformed organizations provide their own training and support systems.

5.   The role of the specialist worker

An increasing number of parishes or clusters of churches are recognizing the value of employing someone to work with children and young families. This may be a trained evangelist such as a Church Army officer or an experienced children's worker.

An employed children's worker will lead and coordinate groups for children and their families, befriend them and support them in difficulty. This will include facilitating training and encouraging new initiatives. Equally important, he or she will be an advocate for children, ensuring that their interests are represented in every part of the church's life, including worship and social events. A number of employed workers have spearheaded new ways of children and their families forming their own Christian communities and worshipping together.

Specialist schools' workers have a slightly different role. Most of them serve a cluster of schools and may be on the staff of a Christian organization such as Scripture Union or the Church Army. They provide a Christian presence in schools similar to that of a chaplain, are involved with worship, RE, circle time and pastoral care. Some of the work may include organizing and leading groups like a Christian Union, a Bible study group, or in secondary schools a *Youth Alpha* or *Emmaus* course. These groups may include a number of children who are interested in or attracted by the Christian faith but are not involved with church in any other way.

Whatever the brief of these workers, they are in the forefront of the Church's mission with children and their families. Recently established training courses for young people considering a career in children's work are a response to the growing demand for professional qualifications commensurate with the responsibilities of the work. Children's work is not an offshoot of youth work but requires different skills.

6.   An environment for creating disciples

Developing a form of church that will last lies in its ethos and structure. *Mission-shaped Church* reminds us of the work of Henry Venn of the Church Missionary Society who campaigned 'for the deliberate foundation of indigenous churches that fitted the culture and were led by local people'.[6] The situation for today's children is not so different. Children need to be part of churches that fit their culture and lifestyles, involve them in decision-making, and encourage them to take responsibility as they mature.

We rejoice as we read the stories of groups of young children worshipping and coming to faith and then bringing along their friends. It has to be faced, however, that many of the successful groups of ten years ago are no longer operating. This may be because a situation has changed, and the focus of the children's ministry has responded accordingly. Some groups close because a leader resigned or was ill, or a key family moved house and the group collapsed.

Other groups are so successful that they have to divide or find other premises. These can be opportunities for even more growth but they can also be the start of problems as the children and their leaders cope with the changes.

If the children being church can be described as 'a body', the underlying structure is the skeleton that holds it together and ensures growth. It is unseen but the body will collapse without it at the first sign of stress or problems.

This is not an argument for a heavy structure but for a constitution that frees up the group: 'handrails, not handcuffs'. Following the law and good practice in childcare is vital. So are using common sense, having contingency plans in case of problems and an eye towards possible changes in the future so that the children know they are secure and that their faith can grow in a stable and loving environment.

7. Arguments against differing forms of church for children

A common reservation about children making their own ways of being church is that they are no longer part of the worshipping community. What will happen to them as they get too old for a particular group? A great deal has been done to encourage children to be involved in Sunday worship: is this reverting to the Sunday school model with its weaknesses as well as its strengths?

The most vocal argument, however, is that the parish church will suffer. It may already be struggling with a small and ageing congregation. If children worship elsewhere, it may not be viable in years to come. This fear is understandable, but it is treating children as 'fish', commodities to be forced into a particular mould for the sake of maintaining a familiar tradition. Deliberately to restrict ways that children can hear the gospel and experience worshipping God in the hope that a few of them may find their way to the traditional Sunday service is unacceptable.

Maintenance before mission

One Christmas Eve the vicar was delighted that so many families had attended the crib service that some people were sitting on the chancel floor and others were standing at the back of the church. The churchwarden, however, had a different view. 'I want it stopped', he said. 'We have had fewer people at Midnight Mass since we started it.'

Children being church is not an either/or situation. Still less is it about destroying or marginalizing the inherited Church. It is recognizing the many ways in which children's worshipping communities are growing alongside the traditional church and are still part of it, just as the early Communion congregation is as much a part of the church as the family service congregation, even if they rarely meet. Indeed, much of what is disparagingly called 'the fringe' is actually a form of church. Children are worshipping God and learning about him in school, in clubs, and midweek worship and so on. Most important, the Christian story is becoming more accessible to the increasing numbers of youngsters who know nothing about the Christian faith.

8. Holding it all together

The image of clusters of children (as well as adults) meeting and worshipping alongside traditional services is attractive as an ideal, but it still presents huge questions:

a.   How do children progress as they grow out of a particular group?

b.   How do we keep a sense of being part of the wider Church?

a. Responding to growth in age and faith

The first question is a major challenge. Sometimes the style of a meeting will change, as the children grow older. This will be the case in a housegroup or similar self-contained unit. Other times, a new group will be formed that is geared towards the older children. This is shown in the story about the Kidz Klub and is currently a major challenge for the growing Praise & Play service.[7] It has huge implications for the provision of leaders, time and money. In some cases, where there is a major demographic change, a group may close because it is no longer sustainable, and the energy will be put into another area of mission.

There is also the issue of young people coming to faith, wishing to be baptized or confirmed, and eventually leaving school and home. There are no easy answers, but this is a strong case for giving priority to the worship of the traditional church in any development. It has to grow alongside the other forms of church so that, should young people feel that this is where they want to be as they grow up (or that there is no other option), they find a viable alternative with worship of a high standard.

b. Forming links with the rest of the Church

On a practical level, anything done in the name of the church is the legal responsibility of the incumbent and the Parochial Church Council. The PCC provides accountability and support, which may seem unnecessary when things are going well, but that ownership is vital to ensure support for everything from providing funding to dealing with a crisis. An effective way of keeping the ministry among children in the mind of the church leaders is to have 'children' as an agenda item at every meeting and see that there is something to report. Other ways of raising the profile of the children include publishing articles and stories in the magazine, involving the local media if something special happens, displaying pictures of events (with parental permission) and welcoming adults to visit the group and join in the worship.

Distributing information about parish services and events to every child is a practical way of reminding them that they are part of a larger local church and may involve families in occasional services and social events.

We have already discussed, in Chapter 9, the value of diocesan events, visiting cathedrals and going on pilgrimage. They serve to remind the children (and their leaders) that there is a huge family of Christian children across the country and beyond. It is known as 'the wider Church' and is part of the communion of saints that embraces every age and race.

Most of all, see that each group prays for the different parts of the Church. Remember the children's groups and the school at the Sunday Eucharist and ask the children to pray for the worship that takes place in the church, the school and the activities for children in the wider community.

These links and many others strengthen the bonds between the new and the inherited forms of church and people of all ages on their Christian journeys. They affirm the diversity of people and ways they worship and seek to follow Christ within the structure of his Church.

Some questions for discussion

1. Have we imposed on children ways of nurturing and worshipping that are inappropriate?

2. How can we develop our liturgy and use it creatively so that it is more inclusive of children?

3. How are children being church beyond Sunday already? What support are they receiving and should it be developed?

4. What children's groups might be developed in the community that could relate to children who are not in contact with church?

5. Are we starting with the children, and putting their needs first, or are we fitting them around our own needs and perceptions?

6. Are our clergy and leaders equipped to respond to the challenges and opportunities presented by reviewing our situation?

11 Conclusion: the children speak for themselves

In July 2005, the General Synod held a debate on children and Holy Communion. It had first given permission for children to be admitted to Holy Communion in 1997, after nearly 30 years of discussion. Now the practice had been reviewed and was discussed again. The atmosphere was warm and accepting as person after person spoke about how children receiving Holy Communion had transformed and enriched their churches, and how their faith and reverence had been an example to everyone. The children themselves had changed people's hearts and minds.

This book attempts to show how children are an integral part of the Church's mission in the world and how a mission-shaped church is for all generations. The real evidence, however, comes from the children and their stories. Every story offers a wide range of experience besides the subject that it is illustrating. Even more striking, however, is the large number of cases in which the children and their worship (which often takes place away from the church building), have had a positive effect on the adult congregation and thereby the whole Church.

The common question about a Church with so much variety and diversity is what will happen in the future? We like to look ahead to see what will happen. We want guarantees of success and long-term commitment from our children.

The number of children and their parents who know the Christian story is still frighteningly low. There is, however, goodwill towards children hearing that story and experiencing worship that was not there ten years ago. Statistics show that churches are reaching large numbers of children through ways apart from Sunday. We must maximize these opportunities and be prepared for changes and surprises along the way. At the same time, those involved in education and liturgical reform need to develop as a matter of urgency forms of worship, including eucharistic worship, for when children are present.

The real battle for children being part of the Church, however, is not about finding workers to lead children's groups or establishing worship that is more accessible, much though they are needed. It is about changing the hearts and minds of adult Christians so that they can share responsibility for the Church's mission among the youngest and most vulnerable generation.

This can best be done by the children themselves. Any church that truly accepts its children as people who matter – fellow disciples with much to give as well as to receive – will always be invigorated and have that hope for the future, not least from the vibrant faith of its youngest members.

Notes

Acknowledgements
1. Published by the Arthur Rank Centre and edited by Jeremy Martineau.

Introduction
1. *Mission-shaped Church*, GS 1523, Church House Publishing, 2004.

Chapter 1
1. *Mission-shaped Church*, GS 1523, Church House Publishing, 2004, p. 2.
2. The figure was 34 per cent in 2002. *Mission-shaped Church*, p. 2.
3. In 1998, the Government started to develop 'Wrap-around childcare' to increase and regulate the provision of registered childminders, breakfast and after-school clubs.
4. In 1994, 4 per cent of children attended an after-school club. By 2002, it was 14 per cent. Source: 4Children (formerly the Kids Club Network).
5. *Mission-shaped Church*, p. 2.
6. *Mission-shaped Church*, p. 3.
7. *Mission-shaped Church*, p. 4.
8. National Statistics online: www.statistics.gov.uk.
9. *The Guardian*, 28 April 2004.
10. *Mission-shaped Church*, p. 4.
11. *Mission-shaped Church*, p. 2.
12. *Protecting All God's Children,* 3rd edn, Church House Publishing, 2004.
13. *The Way Ahead: Church of England schools in the new millennium*, GS 1406, Church House Publishing, 2001.
14. *Mission-shaped Church*, p. 11.
15. UK Christian Handbook, *Religious Trends 2*, 2000/2001.
16. *Mission-shaped Church*, p. 11.
17. *Mission-shaped Church*, p. 2.
18. *Mission-shaped Church*, p. 12.
19. *Mission-shaped Church*, p. 13.
20. *Mission-shaped Church*, p. 14.
21. Bishop of Birmingham; now Archbishop of York.

Chapter 2
1. This became the National Society for Promoting Religious Education.
2. Statement about educational purposes recorded at foundation meeting on 16 October 1811. Source: www.natsoc.org.uk/society/history.
3. An Autobiography, Philip Snowden, I. Nicholson & Watson, 1934.
4. *Mission-shaped Church*, GS 1523, Church House Publishing, 2004, p. 41. Source: UK Christian Handbook, *Religious Trends 2*, 2000/2001.

5. The author possesses a certificate awarded to a relation aged six years, for passing the diocesan divinity exam in 1909.
6. In 1940, 35 per cent of children in the UK attended Sunday school. Source: UK Christian Handbook, *Religious Trends 2*, 2000/2001.
7. *All God's Children?* GS 988, a report from the General Synod Board of Education and Board of Mission, National Society/Church House Publishing,1991, p. 7 section 1.12.
8. *All God's Children?*, 1991, p. 7 section 1.13.
9. Stephen Bigger,'Introduction to Religious Education', Foundations for Religious Education, Westminster College Oxford, 1995.
10. *Mission-shaped Church*, p. 40.
11. Church of England Board of Education, *Children in the Way*, National Society, 1988, p. 69 section 5.36.
12. *Children in the Way*, 1988, pp.84–5, sections 7.26-7.38.
13. *Children in the Way*, 1988, p. 91, sections 4.1, 4.3; p. 92, sections 5.1, 5.4.
14. *All God's Children?*, 1991.
15. *Church Statistics 2003/4*, Church House Publishing, 2005.
16. *Mission-shaped Church*, pp. 40–1.
17. *Mission-shaped Church*, p. 153, note 17.
18. *Children Included*, GS Misc. 804, Church House Publishing, 2005, Chapter 3, sections 8–9.
19. *All God's Children?*, 1991, p. 3 section 1.1.
20. Church of England, Statistics for Mission, Attendance and Membership figures 2001.
21. Church of England, Statistics for Mission, Attendance and Membership figures 2002.
22. Archdeacons' Articles of Enquiry 2004 (figures calculated from the 71 per cent available).
23. www.freshexpressions.org.uk

Chapter 3

1. One example is the banning of Christmas cribs in public places by some local authorities.
2. *Children Included*, GS Misc. 804, Church House Publishing, 2005, Chapter 2 section 5.9.
3. From a paper written for Coventry diocese and available from www.covdioc.webspace.fish.co.uk (site under reconstruction at time of writing).
4. *Mission-shaped Church*, GS 1523, Church House Publishing, 2004, p. 77.
5. *Explorations: Making Sense of Generation Y: The world view of 16- to 25-year-olds*, Church House Publishing, 2006.
6. The British Household Panel Study and Key Issues in Religious Change, 2005.
7. From a University of Manchester web site press release, to be found at www.manchester.ac.uk/press/title,38696,en.htm

8. Church of England Board of Education, *Children in the Way*, National Society, 1988, recommendation, Chapter 4.3, p. 91.
9. BBC Radio 4, 29 August 2005.
10. *Children Included*, 2005.
11. *Mission-shaped Church*, p. 77.

Chapter 4

1. See Chapter 2, section 7.
2. Church of England Board of Education, *Children in the Way*, National Society, 1988, section 3.23.
3. *Children in the Way*, 1988, section 4.3.
4. Roots and Scripture Union provide all-age worship material as part of their teaching programmes.
5. *Children Included*, GS Misc 804, Church House Publishing, 2005, chapters 2 section 5.2; and 4 section 3.3.
6. This story is part of an article by Captain Richard Beadle, first published in 'Spotlight Ireland'. Reproduced with his permission.
7. A fuller article was originally published in *Country Way*, issue 31, published by The Arthur Rank Centre, Autumn 2002.

Chapter 5

1. *Mission-shaped Church,* GS 1523, Church House Publishing, 2004, pp. 35, 42.
2. An in-depth consultancy in five dioceses that forms Key Area 2 of the Church of England's Strategy for Children, Sharing the Good News with Children, GS 1515, Church House Publishing, 2003.
3. *Church Statistics 2003/4*, Church House Publishing, 2005, sections 5, 10.
4. See the stories in Chapter 6, section 3, 'The Lion's Den' and Chapter 9, section 1, 'The conscience of the village'.
5. This sort of development is illustrated in the story 'Barney Bear Club' in Chapter 7, section 2.

Chapter 6

1. Graham Tomlin, *The Provocative Church*, SPCK, 2002, p. 79.
2. Source: Archdeacons' Articles of Enquiry 2004 (figures calculated from the 71 per cent available).
3. Originally published on the Fresh Expressions web site: www.freshexpressions.org.uk Reproduced with permission.

Chapter 8

1. *Mission-shaped Church*, GS 1523, Church House Publishing, 2004, p. 8, 67–9.
2. *Mission-shaped Church*, pp. 67–8.
3. *The Way Ahead: Church of England schools in the new millennium*, GS 1406, Church House Publishing, 2001, sections 3.10; 3.11.

4. *The Way Ahead*, 2001, section 3.4.
5. Originally published on the Fresh Expressions website: www.freshexpressions.org.uk. Reproduced with permission.
6. Emmaus resources are produced by Church House Publishing; see www.e-mmaus.org.uk for further details.
7. See Margaret Withers, *Where are the Children?*, BRF, 2005, chapter 14, for a strategic plan.

Chapter 10

1. *Mission-shaped Church*, GS 1523, Church House Publishing, 2004, chapter 6, p. 106.
2. Margaret Withers, *Not Just Sunday: Setting up and running midweek clubs for children*, Church House Publishing, 2002, p. 2.
3. See Chapter 5, section 2.
4. Mary K. Stone, published by Religious and Moral Education Press (SCM/Canterbury Press). See Further information and reading.
5. GS Misc 804, 2005.
6. *Mission-shaped Church*, p. 121.
7. See Chapters 6, section 4, and 4, section 8.

Further information and reading

General information

Most dioceses have a children's adviser. Every diocese has a missioner, and sometimes an evangelist or a parish development officer. They will work alongside a parish and will know of local examples of good practice. Organizations connected with children's activities and liturgical committees may provide useful advice.

Christian organizations concerned with children and evangelism

BRF: www.brf.org.uk

Church Army: www.churcharmy.org.uk

Children Worldwide: www.childrenworldwide.co.uk

Church Mission Society: www.cms-uk.org

CPAS: www.cpas.org.uk

Crusaders: www.crusaders.org.uk

CURBS: www.curbsproject.org.uk

Fresh Expressions: www.freshexpressions.org.uk

Rural Sunrise: www.ruralmissions.org.uk/sunrise.htm

Scripture Union: www.scriptureunion.org.uk

Further reading

Children and childhood

Kathryn Copsey, *From the Ground Up*, BRF, 2005.

G. Miles and J. Wright (eds), *Celebrating Children*, Paternoster, 2003.

J. and R. Mills (eds), *Childhood Studies*, Routledge, 2000.

Children and worship

Nick Harding, *Top Tips on All Age Worship*, Scripture Union, 2005.

Diana Murrie, *Baptism Cube*, Church House Publishing, 2006.

Diana Murrie, *Communion Cube*, Church House Publishing, 2002.

Diana Murrie, *My Baptism Book*, Church House Publishing, 2006.

Diana Murrie, *My Communion Book*, Church House Publishing, 2002.

B. Pedley and J. Muir, *Children in the Church?*, National Society/Church House Publishing, 1997.

Neil Pugmire, *Launchpad*, BRF, 2004.

Margaret Withers, *The Gifts of Baptism*, BRF, 2003.

Margaret Withers, *Welcome to the Lord's Table* (revised edn), BRF, 2006.

Children being church

P. Clarke and G. Pearson, *Kidz Klubs: the Alpha of Children's Evangelism?*, Grove, 1998.

Penny Frank, *Whole in One*, CPAS, 2005.

Mike Law, *Small Groups Growing Churches*, Scripture Union, 2003.

Janet Marshall, *Special People, Special Places*, BRF, 2005.

Philip Mountstephen, *Body Beautiful?*, Grove, 2005.

Margaret Withers, *Not Just Sunday*, Church House Publishing, 2002.

Margaret Withers, *Where Two or Three . . .*, Church House Publishing, 2004.

Church of England reports

Children in the Midst, GS Misc. 788, Church House Publishing, 2005.

Children Included, GS Misc. 804, Church House Publishing, 2005.

Mission-shaped Church, GS 1523, Church House Publishing, 2004.

Sharing the Good News with Children, GS 1515, Church House Publishing, 2003.

Club programmes

Kathryn Copsey, *Colours of Easter*, BRF, 2005.

Claire Gibb, *Building New Bridges*, Church House Publishing, 1996.

Dave Godfrey, *Pyramid Rock* (holiday club), Scripture Union, 2005.

Mark Griffiths, *Fuzion – programme,* Monarch, 2002,

Mark Griffiths, *Impact –* programme, Monarch, 2003.

Murray McBride, *Walking with Jesus for Advent and Christmas,* BRF, 2005.

Neil Pugmire, *The Adventures of the J Team*, BRF, 2003.

Eleanor Zuercher, *Not Sunday, Not School!,* BRF, 2006.

Evangelism among children

Penny Frank, *Every Child: a Chance to Choose*, CPAS, 2002.

Helen Franklin, *Top Tips on Reaching Unchurched Children*, Scripture Union, 2005.

David Gatward, *Mission Possible*, Scripture Union, 2001.

Margaret Withers, *Where are the Children?*, BRF, 2005.

Schools

Margaret Goldthorpe, *Stay Cool in School,* BRF, 2003.

John Guest, *Collective Worship Unwrapped*, BRF, 2005.

Lee Jackson, *Effective Schools Work*, Kingsway, 2003.

Brian Ogden, *Maximus Mouse and Friends*, Scripture Union, 2001.

Brian Ogden, *Year Round Assemblies*, BRF, 2002.

Gillian Wood, *Linking Churches and Schools,* Churches Together in England, 2003.

Spirituality

Gill Ambrose, *The 'E' Book*, National Society/Church House Publishing, 2000.

Jerome W. Berryman, *Godly Play*, Augsburg, 1991.

Francis Bridger, *Children Finding Faith*, Scripture Union, 2000.

J. M. Eibner and S. G. Walker, *God, Kids and Us*, Morehouse, 1997.

Anthony Ewens and Mary K. Stone, *Teaching about God, Worship and Spirituality*, Religious and Moral Education Press, 2001.

Anthony Ewens and Mary K. Stone, *Teaching about Jesus*, Religious and Moral Education Press, 2001.

Jill Fuller, *Looking Beyond*, Kevin Mayhew, 1996.

Mary K. Stone, *Don't Just Do Something: Sit There!*, Religious and Moral Education Press, 1997.

Young children

Jane Farley, Eileen Goddard and Judy Jarvis, *Under Fives – Alive and Kicking!* Church House Publishing, 1998.

Janet Gaukroger, *Sharing Jesus with Under Fives*, Crossway, 1994.

Patricia Beall Gavigan, *Talking Together: Exploring the Christian Year with Under Fives*, Cassell, 1996.

Vicki Howie, *Easy Ways to Bible Fun for the Very Young*, BRF, 2001.

Ro Willoughby, *My Big Red Book: Outlines for Pre-schools*, Scripture Union, 2001.

Ro Willoughby, *My Little Red Book: First Steps in Bible Reading*, Scripture Union, 2001.

Index